ABANDON YOURSELVES TOTALLY TO ME

Meditations
by Fr. Tomislav Vlašić and Fr. Slavko Barbarić
from January to June 1985

MILAN 1985

This book is available from:

IRELAND:
GERALD MORE
31 Pinewood Park - Rathfarnham, Dublin 14 - Tel. 932883

SCOTLAND:
CRAIG LODGE
Dalmally, Argylishire, PA33 1AR - Scotland - Tel. (083 82) 216

ENGLAND & WALES:
JOHN MAC MAHON
70 Merrivale Road - Rising Brook - Stafford ST 17 9EE - Tel. (0785) 47897

CANADA:
Sr. DANIELA A. ORAZZO
St. Theresa's Day Care Centre Carmelite Missionary Sisters
1196 Wilson Ave - Downsview, Ont. M3M 1H3
Tel. (416) 6366123 - 6381560

U.S.A.
TERESA MANAX
407 West Oak Street - West, Texas 76691 - Tel. (817) 826-3721

THE RIEHLE FOUNDATION
FRANCES and BILL RECK
P.O. Box 7 - Milford, Ohio 45150 - Tel. (513) 831-8068

The Association of the Friends of Medjugorje
20123 Milan (Italy) - Via Nirone 9

TO MARY QUEEN OF PEACE
with love from her children
of the Milan and Lecco groups

« Our Lady is speaking to the world:
we must therefore acknowledge her as
a precious gift given to us by God, to
be accepted, and to be lived.
And it is very important to understand
that it is not a question of a general
veneration for Our Lady.
Here we are offered a special gift, a
special love, a special grace which we
must accept in order to become filled with
richness, in order to be saved »

(Fr. Tomislav Vlašić, 24th May, 1985)

Milan, 14th September, 1985

INDEX

INTRODUCTION

The aim of this volume is to carry on the work of spreading the Medjugorje messages which we started to do in the previous book « Open your hearts to Mary Queen of Peace ».

Here we are dealing with the spiritual path during the first six months of 1985 through the meditations of Father Tomislav Vlašić and Father Slavko Barbarić.

Readers will also find some news of the chain of events, as recounted by the Fathers.

The texts have been transcribed from recordings, leaving out only some parts which were merely repetitions of information or messages.

On the other hand, we have again brought forward those messages whose various comments could inspire further reflection.

After the meditations, we have listed the messages given to the Medjugorje Parish by Our Lady every Thursday, or on particular feast days, from the beginning (1st March, 1984) up to and including June, 1985.

The translation from the Croat into Italian was made by Mirjana Vasilj Zuccarini.

Alberto Bonifacio - Mario Brughera

There may be some inaccuracies in the text due both to the fact that the Yugoslav Fathers found some difficulty in expressing themselves in Italian, and that they were unable to correct the proofs.

The editors therefore assume full responsibility for the transcriptions and in every case they can guarantee the authenticity of the texts.

MEDITATIONS BY FATHER TOMISLAV VLAŠIĆ
AND FATHER SLAVKO BARBARIĆ

The main message is this: the presence of Our Lady

I am sure you have already heard and read much in newspapers and books about Medjugorje. The thing I must tell you always is what is happening to the visonaries. Every evening they have visions. Our Lady is giving an account of her life in Nazareth to Vicka, and Vicka writes it down every evening after the vision. But she (Vicka) cannot tell us anything yet. One day it will all be published and will be of great interest.

To Ivanka, Our Lady talks of the problems of the world and of the Church, and when she gives her permission, this will also be published. It is still a secret for us. A few days ago, when asked by an Italian television group « What can you tell the people? », Ivanka replied: « Do as Our Lady says, be converted; there is not much time. »

We do not know what Ivanka has seen, what she knows, but when we speak of the problems of the world and of the Church, there is a real need for conversion as we all know.

Ivan, Marija and Jakov see Our Lady every evening and speak to her, they pray and commend the sick to her. Our Lady gives the messages through them and more especially through Marija.

Every Thursday, since the beginning of Lent last year, there has been a message for us, for the Parish and for all the pilgrims.

Recently we repeated some medical tests on the visionaries with some doctors who came with Father Laurentin. First they tested the brain and the heart (arterial pressure). Last week they tested the children's eyes and hearing. What can be said about these experiments? Scientifically it cannot be demonstrated that the visionaries see Our Lady, but these tests help us to see and also to understand what is happening to the visionaries bodies, brains, eyes and hearing. All these tests show that something extraordinary is happening.

We can see that interest in this phenomenon is growing day by day. The doctors from Louvain (Belgium) for instance said, after watching a recording of the event (they were all agnostic): «You cannot say there is nothing there.» When an agnostic speaks like that, it really means something.

These phenomena are very simple. There is nothing strange about them. The visionaries start praying and at a certain moment, as if they had been struck, they kneel down and we can hear nothing more. We can only see their lips move and their eyes stare. After a few minutes, they are saying the Our Father – they say that Our Lady starts it – and in the end they say «Ode»: She is gone, She is leaving.

During the vision, they do not react to the strongest light. Once a member of the Commission who was in the Chapel pricked Vicka, but she did not react. The Parish priest also tried seizing Jakov by his hair, but he did not react either.

There were many similar instances.

They do not realise how long the visions last; they are out of time and space.

After the encephalogram, the doctors could state that it was not a case of epilepsy, or of hallucination or even of a dream. So they are in a state of wakefulness, but on the other hand do not react as they would normally if they are awake. The test on the eyes shows a simultaneous reaction, they all begin staring at something we cannot see, at the same instant.

The doctors gave Ivan and Ivanka a headset to generate and measure the intensity of sound. At first, before the apparition, the doctors kept it very low. During the apparition, they made it ninety, the highest decibel level but Ivan did not hear anything. He told me: «At first, there seemed to be a tractor, an engine inside my head,» but during the apparition – when the measured noise was at its highest – he didn't hear anything.

The doctor told me that a normal head could not stand such a noise level. They also wanted to make a throat test too, to see why their voices couldn't be heard while they were speaking to Our Lady, but they have not yet done it.

Another thing I must tell you is this: Vicka had an operation about a month ago for appendicitis and something else, but nothing special. She is well now and comes to Church every evening.

The main message is this: The PRESENCE OF OUR LADY.

For nearly four years, Our Lady has been appearing every evening. She appears to the visionaries where they happen to be. The apparitions are not affected by place or even time: where they are, Our Lady appears.

Vicka told me that during the operation, Our Lady appeared to her for twelve minutes in the operating-theatre. An hour after the operation Vicka was still under the influence of the anaesthetic. A young man who had gone with her to Zagreb was in the hospital room and was present during the vision, and he told me: « If I had had a video-recorder and if I could have recorded this apparition, we would have had the final answer for all those who wonder if it is possible or not, for all those who are in doubt. »

Under the anaesthetic, Vicka could not speak, her eyes were closed. Suddenly she awoke and began reacting as she usually did during the apparitions, praying to Our Lady as usual, but after the apparition, she was again under the anaesthetic. This message of Our Lady's presence is not only for Vicka, but for all of us. Our Lady shows herself as a mother and voices the truth of the Second Vatican Council's declaration that she is the « Mother of the Church. » And the Mother belongs to the Church, belongs to the children. We have heard many times in the messages that Our Lady is our Mother; that she wants us all in peace, to be reconciled, to pray, to seek Jesus.

In a message through Jelena, she said: « *If you knew how much I love you, you would weep for joy.* » Another message through Jelena was this: « *If there is someone before you asking for something, you give it to him: I stand before so many hearts that do not open to me. Pray that the world may accept my love.* » We can also say this: Our Lady comes to every family, to the Church, to the world and wants to lead us to Jesus. But she does not compel anybody, she invites us. To all those who have heard and follow her, Our Lady says: « *Pray that the world may accept my love.* » So she has put the future of the world partly into the hands of those of us who have started praying. She says: « *Pray that the world may accept my love.* »

It is very important. Accepting Our Lady as our Mother also means consecrating oneself. All of us consecrated ourselves to the Sacred Heart of Mary on 25th March when the Pope asked for the consecration of the whole world. Consecrating oneself means just this: accepting Our Lady as the Mother, accepting her in the family, accepting her in every sphere of life.

How does she behave with the visionaries? She behaves as she does with every one of us. What Our Lady can do depends on us. For example, she said to the visionaries: « *I would like you to go into a convent. You must make up your own minds. I will help you in your decisions.* »

You can see how free she leaves them. I am sure I can say it is like that with us all. Our Lady invites us to peace, to love and reconciliation, but she cannot give us love or reconciliation if we do not look for them. She said once in a message: « *You are a chosen people, but you are not yet aware of what Our Lord gives you and I can only say this to you: Pray, pray, pray to be able to understand in prayer the immense love I have for you and Our Lord's love.* »

It is a very important message.

The first thing this message says is: « *you are a chosen people.* » We are chosen, but we do not understand what it means to be chosen and loved by Our Lord and Our Lady, we will never understand...

Above all, these apparitions are a sign for us that we are a chosen people; and who can understand this love which has been showing itself in this way for more than forty two months?

Another thing: Our Lady said: « *Pray; without prayer you cannot understand love.* » Prayer is living with Someone and through life with Him learning how to love Him and accept his love. One last thing is this: Our Lady said: « *I have only this to say to you: Pray, pray, pray.* » This means that Our Lady is acting like a mother who has prepared a big meal with special food and invites us. But we come to the house complaining: « We have no peace, we are frightened, we are thirsty, we are hungry... » and Our Lady says: « Look I have prepared everything, but it is up to you. I can do no more than say: Come, eat your fill, drink. »

In these messages and these events, we can see both Our Lord's great love for us and the hardness of our hearts. So many times Our Lady has said: « *But you still do not follow me, you still do not understand.* » You can understand this as a form of teaching: Our Lady brings us up; and yet on the same day at the same time, a mother can reproach her child and also offer him some chocolate saying « Come, let's eat it together. »

We also hear that Our Lady always thanks us in the messages. At the end of the message there is always the same sentence. Marija says that Our Lady always ends by saying « *Thank you for responding to my call.* »

So Our Lady acts just like a mother who wants to teach her children about peace and love and these two things are the hardest to learn.

The messages before Christmas can be reduced to a single phrase: « *You do not yet know how to love. I am your Mother and I have come to teach you to love.* » And who can say: « I have loved, I have finished learning about love? » Who can say: « I love everybody? » Who can say: « I loved yesterday, today I needn't do it? » Love is another word for conversion, another word for peace. You can learn about love and understand it, Our Lady said, only when you start praying, when you start fasting.

Yesterday – it was Thursday – Our Lady said: « *At this time, the Lord has granted you many graces. I invite you to make this a thanksgiving week for all of you. Give thanks.* »

In response to this message, we gave thanks during the adoration of the Eucharist, and we will do so again this evening (because every Friday, we adore the Cross). At Christmas time, we are going

15

to worship before the crib. But again we want to give thanks. Our Lady asked us to do so for the whole week and on 2nd January she said, through Ivan, that several plans, several projects have been accomplished.

So she asks for thanksgiving. I asked Ivan what had been accomplished, but he did not answer. Ivan had a vision on the mountain this week and said: « I have been seeing Our Lady for more than three years, but I have never seen her as glad and happy as tonight. » Our Lady told us through him to give thanks. She told us this because some plans have been accomplished.

On Thursday before Christmas, she said: « *From now on every day until Christmas I wish every family to bring a flower as a sign of abandonment to the Lord.* »

She told us to do something concrete for Jesus: « *Bring flowers, as a sign of your trust, of your love.* » The flowers were put by the crib. Our Lady said: « *When Jesus comes, may He see your trust and stay.* » In fact this was what we did: we spoke to all the families about this and said: « Bring a flower on Christmas Eve. We will ask Our Lady to bless all the flowers you take home afterwards. » Through Jelena, Our Lady explained the spiritual meaning of the flowers. She said: « *You must be flowers that never fade.* » [*]

I know that a lot of people have resolved to go on with the monthly confession, to come to the adoration on Thursdays, to pray and meditate.

All this is happening to teach us. Our Lady wants to teach us. We do not know when the apparitions will stop, but the school of love can never end, and the school of peace can never end. So by coming here you become responsible for peace in your hearts, in your families and also all over the world. You must never forget, not even during the liturgy during Mass when you cannot understand our language, that you, by coming here, by your prayers, are going

---

[*] Message for Christmas through Jelena Vasilj: « *It is my wish that you may be the flower that blooms at Christmas for Jesus. The flower that will not fade when Christmas is over. I wish your hearts to be the shepherds of Jesus.* »

with Our Lady every day on her most extraordinary earthly journey – a journey one could never have imagined.

Our Lady asks for the Creed, seven Our Fathers', Hail Mary's and Glory be's, the entire Rosary, prayer, monthly confession and two days of fasting.

There is no substitute for fasting and prayer. You must begin as you can and go on. Personal visions have always been granted throughout the history of the Church when something important has been forgotten. The visions come to remind us of it. For example, we have given up prayer and fasting, saying that we no longer have time, we cannot fast. We have said we can give a little money to others, but not fast. But Jesus fasted, the Mother of God, the Virgin, fasted, all the prophets, the saints and especially St. Francis of Assisi fasted.

So Our Lady gives new value to prayer and fasting because she wants us to live the Gospel.

(Fr. Slavko Barbarić - 4th January, 1985)

« The family must pray together and read the Bible »

At this time of January, after Christmas, we could say that all Our Lady's messages spoke of satan: beware of satan, satan is strong, he is angry, he wants to destroy my plans... *

And She asked everyone to pray for all those who were tempted. Each one of us is tempted, but above all, the people responsible for these events. So it is necessary to pray hard. A fortnight ago She said: *« Pray so that all the trials that come from satan might serve for the glory of the Lord »*. She also said that it was easier to disarm satan with ardent prayers and humble love. These are the arms to use to disarm Satan without any difficulty. We must not be afraid. So pray and love with humility, just like Our Lady prayed and loved.

Last Thursday (14th February) She said: *« I am sad because there are still many who are not following this path, even in the Parish. »* And She also said: *« You must pray in your families and you must read the Bible. »*

I have already remarked at other times that we do not come across many messages where Our Lady says *« you must »*. This is what She said to Marija, « you must. »

The messages of the apparitions are always an invitation — « if you wish. » But this time She said *« you must. »* I think She also

---

* In January, the Madonna delivered this message through Vicka (14th January, 1985): *« My dear children. Satan is so powerful that he wishes, with all his strength, to obstruct my plans which I started with you. Pray, only pray and never stop, not even for a second. I shall pray My Son that all the plans I have started will be accomplished. Be patient and persevere in your prayers and do not let satan discourage you. He acts very strongly in the world. Be careful! »*

wanted to prepare us for Lent. For example, if a mother takes a three-year old child by the hand to teach him to walk, at a certain moment she will let go of his hand and say: « You must walk alone... » It is not a command. He has grown and so she says: « Now you must, because you can. »

We can say this because little Jelena, who has internal locutions, explained the difference between Our Lady's way of speaking and that of satan. (She has at times heard and has been tried by satan.)

Jelena said that Our Lady never says: « You must » and She does not anxiously wait to see what will happen. She offers, She invites, She lets us be free.

On the contrary, when satan proposes anything or looks for something, he is nervous, he does not wait, he has no time: he wants everything immediately, he is impatient.

And so I think that if Our Lady says: « *You must,* » then we really must!

We shall see what Our Lady says this evening.

Every day there is something, or a message for us...

You see, the general message is not peace, it is Our Lady's presence. If She has not said anything, if, for example She has only appeared for a second, it is the general message: « *I am with you.* »

And from Her presence everything receives a special force.

(Fr. Slavko Barbarić - 21st February, 1985)

To fast means to open up to the Lord

...Fasting is compulsory for us all according to the Gospel, the same as prayer. Jesus said that his disciples used to fast.

When the Pharisees went to Jesus and said: why is it that John's disciples fast and yours do not? Jesus replied: « Can the wedding guests mourn as long as the bridegroom is with them? The days will come, when the bridegroom is taken away from them, and then they will fast. »

Jesus has been taken away, but has Risen and we live « already and not yet » in this tension of the Kingdom of God. We are in expectation, we are waiting. The Church prays for the coming of the Lord and fasting, amongst other things, has an eschatological dimension. I await: for one day I do not want to eat; I am waiting for my Lord. This is an eschatological dimension and the Lord has spoken for his disciples. There is a particular manner of evil which can only be driven out by prayer and fasting. The disciples were unable to act because they had not fasted.

I have said this as a general principle. I do not know anyone in the Church who can forbid a Christian to pray and to fast. If the practice of the Church is reduced to a minimum, this is according to the situation: as, for example, eating one hour before taking Communion.

Many wanted to take Communion before going to work, but had first to eat. Otherwise they would have to go without anything for the whole day. So the Church said: we will do it in this way. Jesus had eaten and immediately after the Supper He had Communion with the Apostles; the Church has made a practice now, She has introduced another and can introduce yet another... Fasting is the same thing. There has been a boom in these last years. Many people could not fast and the practice has become somewhat superficial. Our Lady now says: « fast. » She wants to put into practice once more the general principle of the Gospel, of all prophets, of all the Saints who have all fasted. Without doubt Our Lady used to fast, I believe, twice a week because they used to fast for two days in the primitive Church. And if Our Lady says: « you should fast, » She is not saying anything new. She is inviting us to the renewal of a practice.

Fasting is connected with faith. To fast does not mean to be hungry. To fast means to open to the Lord.

He who fasts opens up; someone who fasts is open, he becomes poor in spirit like Our Lady.

And someone poor can never say to another: « I do not need you », because he has a need of the other. I have nothing. He has something, in a material sense. I cannot say: « I have no need of you. Why do I have to ask every day? »

Somebody poor in spirit cannot become an atheist because he sees he needs the Lord, so then if Our Lady now begins a new school of faith, in this world full of atheism, She must invite us to fasting because fasting helps us to open up, to become transparent, to leave a distinct place, also in our body, for the Word. The Holy Fathers of the Church fasted and used to say that fasting is the prayer of the body.

So the body prepares itself, also by fasting, to accept the Lord. And this is to assist our faith.

So, generally speaking, if I see a person genuinely fasting and that it is resulting in no good one must look for another means. But to say that this tradition has disappeared or that one does not fast any more, this is not true. To say that only taking bread and water for a day is harmful, I do not believe it.

Ask your doctor: a doctor will tell you that to abstain from eating for a day is good for your system. It gives a rest to your stomach...

Do we not fear remaining without vitamins only in religious practices? There are so many of us who have an abundance of vitamins and do not know really what to do with them.

If we Christians are afraid of feeling a little hungry for one day, what must we think of all those who are dying every day of hunger in the world?

By feeling a little hungry for a day: we will be better conscious of their cry.

Our Lady does not want us to be lacking in vitamins but wishes for harmony in our lives. In fasting we experience also a new sense of time to discern the important things from those less important. Many, after having started fasting have realized that it was not necessary to sit in front of the television every evening.

If for an evening nobody eats, smokes or drinks in a household this often means a healthy home.

From statistics: people watch television in France for 18 hours a week, that is three hours a day: but if you begin fasting you will not do this any more.

(Fr. Slavko Barbarić - 21st February, 1985)

« When you are humble, when you pray fervently and when you love, satan cannot even draw close »

Welcome. I wish to thank all those who pray for Medjugorje and for Our Lady's intentions, very much.

I can only say a few words to you as you will hear all the news in Medjugorje. Father Slavko follows the visionaries and the events. I sometimes go to steal a word or two for myself. I shall try to express some reflections about what Our Lady says and from what we have experienced.

I was pleased when I heard that this group has come on a penance pilgrimage, as Lent is about to begin. This morning I shall take advantage of what is happening to speak about today's liturgical texts; for, if we understand the texts, we can understand Lent. The texts are simple. God places life and goodness in front of us, or, if we wish, wickedness and death.

We must choose: living Lent intensely means making a profound choice, a continuous choice. Penance is of use to us in order to return to God, to return to life, to live profoundly, to possess life. Not only do we at once think of life after death (that too), but we begin to live happily here when we are with Our Father, with Our God.

My wish is that we begin Lent, not as a time that will come to an end, but as a stage on our journey, so that after Lent we may be closer to God and we may go all the more swiftly towards God. And in this way, all the events here in Medjugorje will serve us to go swiftly towards God.

I would also like to take the opportunity to say to this group of penance pilgrims that those who want to follow Medjugorje must struggle. We can no longer follow Medjugorje out of curiosity or because of superficial enthusiasm.

Lent shows us that those who want to live Lent must follow it and really live it. Those who want to live Easter must enter the garden of olives. I do not know if any of you have sweated blood. We are called, to enter into this event in life, really, struggle. I tell you this because of our experiences here in Medjugorje. We have realised that this is the time of struggle. People are aware of the struggle. They read about events in the newspapers. There is a deeper interior struggle which we must understand when we read the newspapers where Medjugorje is attacked. While seeing the enemies in the papers we should also become aware of their existence within us; the resistance we meet in the Church and in Christianity is our resistance. Instead of fighting the papers, we should fight in our inner selves. Some people are enraged when they read a newspaper or an article on Medjugorje: in this way the battle is lost. Here is an opportunity to fight, to join in; and this is an opportunity for us all to live reality. We can proceed and deepen our lives. We are called to struggle to the end. We must meditate on this struggle. It is a struggle to the death, to Calvary, as in to-day's Gospel: « he who wants to follow Jesus must renounce everything, he must go through the passion. He will be thrown out also by the High Priests. »

We must be ready to die, but not to die just anyhow, but to die loving. Before dying Jesus forgave everyone. During His life there was no bitterness. Throughout His walk towards Calvary it was always Resurrection. Life in Jesus' heart was never extinguished. When Judas kissed Him, Jesus did not condemn him, but called him « friend », He called him friend.

Jesus gave Himself up to the others. He did not allow a human struggle. He told Peter not to take the sword.

Afterwards a beautiful thing happened: the Apostles ran away, but these men full of fear, have been chosen as the foundation of the Church. St. Peter denied Jesus, but Jesus placed him at the head of the Church.

These are wonderful things whereas we are ready to cast aside and disregard those who offend us. Jesus avails Himself of weak men and on his way to Calvary consoles others.

In his life, in the most difficult situations, there was Resurrection. Jesus' life is not death; He entered death like an underground river to re-emerge. This is the meaning of the Resurrection. We must be ready to die for God, always walking forwards, always increasing our love.

In this struggle against satan which has been pointed out to us by Our Lady in these last few months, Our Lady has given us very precise weapons.

In Medjugorje we have had several struggles with satan and have seen the different means he uses to attack people. Tepid people become indifferent, active people become lethargic and lack their sense of responsibility. So, in this case, he is acting with great cunning.

We have experienced the attacks of satan when he attacked people during Communion by bringing horrid fantasies into their minds and causing them to want to spit on the Host, to blaspheme. We felt a pressure on the congregation as we prayed, like a force pulling us away from prayer.

We have also experienced physical attacks on people, and threats. A lady told us that while she was reciting the Rosary she heard a voice saying: « Enough of this prayer, throw away your rosary. » She continued praying « with an interior sweetness » and this unpleasant voice kept on repeating: « Enough of this prayer! » While she was holding her rosary tightly she felt a hand that was trying to tear it away from her. She held on to it even more tightly and finally that other hand managed to remove the Crucifix and destroy it, but she continued to pray with sweetness feeling an even stronger strength.

I am telling you this so that you know whoever wants to go forward in prayer, in the struggle, will also be tempted in this way. We are lucky because Our Lady always warned us of satan's attacks and told us how to overcome him. She gave us three strong weapons:

HUMILITY, FERVENT PRAYER AND LOVE FOR ONE ANOTHER.

HUMILITY. Do not count on human strength in any way, do not

count on man, not even on Christian ideology, not even on the best men in the Church. Be always humble in front of God.

Our Lady wants us to be ever humble before God and to rely on His strength because human strength fails; in this way, Divine Grace will strengthen us in our trials.

FERVENT PRAYER. Several times She has said: « *Only with prayer can you defeat him.* »

AND LOVE FOR ONE ANOTHER. Where the enemies or opponents of Medjugorje are concerned, Our Lady always tells us to treat them lovingly and with a smile, so that when they see our faces full of love and joy they will be disarmed. This is the method which Our Lady tells us to follow: « *when you are humble, when you pray fervently and when you love all those around you, satan cannot even draw close to you.* »

Do not forget this: when you are humble, when you pray fervently, when you love everybody, satan can not even draw near you. This is important!

On one occasion Our Lady gave a group a task: every member had to act with love and willingness accepting everything, even difficulties. During the day everyone started out to accept all their difficulties with love, with a smile, and at the end of the day when Our Lady appeared, She said, with a smile: « *My dear children, if you only knew how satan fled to-day.* »

So as you see, the struggle against satan is a prevention – when the body has resistance it will not fall ill.

In the same way, satan cannot approach a person who is humble, who loves and prays fervently. This is the road we must follow. The trials will be harder, but through these trials Our Lady wants to purify us and She has told us: « *Through these trials you will be closer to God.* » I want to tell you that you and all the pilgrims must accept these trials, otherwise all the events will come to an end and will not reap the fruits for us desired by Our Lady.

We are entering a phase of purification of the world. The world cannot be purified if it continues in its lethargy and if it does not place itself at God's disposal, with fervent prayer. It will, however, be tempted in an active way by satan.

Remember what happened to St. Anthony the Abbot. A monk saw satan, in a vision, stretched out on the walls of Alexandria, in Egypt, observing the city. Around St. Anthony's cell there were many demons. So the monk said to one of them: « You ought to be ashamed of yourselves, there are so many of you around this cell and there is only one of you lying out on the walls of the city. » And the demon replied: « It is easier for him than all of us around this saint. »

Temptations increase as life progresses, both in people and in the Church. People become stronger. St. Anthony did not fear even a thousand demons, for he was stronger.

On the other hand, one sleeping demon alone was enough on the walls of the city which lived on its sleepiness and in darkness of faith.

And in this way our present times can be understood.

I would like all pilgrims to be able to accept the stage of Lent as a prolonged journey so that Our Lady's messages may be fulfilled. I have spoken a little about the aspect of the struggle – do not worry. Fighting satan is wonderful. It is only necessary to safeguard the peace Our Lady spoke about: humility, love and prayer... It is as exciting as when young people discover new horizons.

And we must not worry because Our Lady sees all and will show us what to do.

I wish to relate two episodes.

When it was snowing and it was very cold Our Lady told the visionaries during the apparition: « *Wear something on your knees tomorrow otherwise you will catch cold.* »

This is a wonderful thought, for it shows us how Our Lady cares also about the little things, about our well-being. It is important.

Another touching moment was the day before yesterday. When the prayer group got together, Our Lady said: « *This evening we will not say our prayers as you must go and enjoy yourselves with the others. Tomorrow we will begin our penance.* »

You can see how Our Lady observes every moment of our lives, She follows us and helps us along our path.

It is extremely important to follow Our Lady with faith and to do all She tells us.

When you go to Medjugorje to pray to-day you will receive a great deal of interior strength. I would like these days, right up to Saturday, to be, for you, the beginning of a new stage to climb up higher, so that when you return home you may be able to tell other pilgrims that they must start on a new journey and not to be discouraged. But we must all know that when satan gets cross we must be strong and not to be frightened. We must rejoice and continue along our path. If we meet any difficulties we must move on in peace, in joy and in prayer.

At this point I would like to stress something important which we ought to learn: active obedience in the Church.

It is extremely dangerous to look on certain instructions passively. As members of the Church we must be actively obedient through prayer and we must be on the alert all the time to do what God wants us to at every particular moment. We must not give up in times of difficulty. We have to spread the truth everywhere and not simply wait for an answer (for example from the official Church), we must spread the light that is within us. At different times in history, when apparitions took place in the Church, the people believed in the event. They obeyed passively...

We are called to pray fervently so that through our prayers and love we may spread the truth.

We must speak with love and prayer.

I would be a liar if I denied that I have lived through an experience, or that I have seen you this morning.

Passive obedience could also be a lie. We must speak with love and pray and we must not forget that truth and love are bound together. We must love, be patient, avoid criticism and yet never give up. Many people are disappointed and this passive obedience is the worst thing that can befall them.

(Fr. Tomislav Vlašić - 22nd February, 1985)

This is the time of decision

... this is the latest message (21st February). I admit that we are a little puzzled by this message: « *Dear children, day after day I have invited you to a re-awakening and to prayer in the Parish, but you have not responded. To-day I invite you for the last time. Now that it is Lent: you may be moved into action for love of this call of mine. If you are not, I no longer wish to give you my messages. God allows me to do this. Thank you for responding to my call.* »
Marija only said what God's word asks of us. God's word always invites and leads us to crossroads where decisions are made. I understand this message in this sense: this is the time of decision. To begin with Our Lady asked for the Creed. The Creed means to make up one's mind. Our Lady urges once again at this time. It is a word which calls for decision: deciding for the Lord.
When Our Lady says: « your Parish », She does not think only of this Parish. For Her, Parish means the whole world.
Yesterday evening I prayed to the Lord: « Lord, perhaps tomorrow you will find someone who will listen to You: keep on speaking to him. »

(Fr. Slavko Barbarić - 23rd February, 1985)

« I am with you and I am your Mother »

Lately things have been as usual. All five visionaries have apparitions. Our Lady is still telling Vicka the story of her life, but Vicka
told me: « I think it will soon end. » Vicka had said this also last
year, as Fr. Tomislav had told us. So Our Lady is telling the story of
her life in short episodes. We do not know when it will end. She
has not told Vicka this yet. But once She has finished we will be
able to publish this story of Our Lady's life. Vicka says that she
writes everything down but she cannot let us see or check anything.
At the moment Vicka is suffering from a benign tumour between
the brain and the cerebellum which cannot be operated upon.
However, it is not growing and therefore it is not a malignant
tumour; it makes her feel very unwell especially when the weather
changes. The pressure effects the tumour and Vicka is in pain,
sometimes for ten minutes, sometimes for half an hour or even an
hour and after, when it is all over, it seems to her that she is
perfectly well. She has told me that during these last few days she
has been unable to sleep at right. Nothing can be done. I said to
her: « look here, we are responsible, we must see a doctor. »
But Vicka replied: « There is no need. » She knows what it is and
she accepts this suffering. This drawing closer to the Cross, to
suffering, and not recoiling from pain is, for Archbishop Franić,
one of the surest proofs that Our Lady speaks to the visionaries.
Vicka prays and fasts a great deal. When somebody asks her how
she feels, she replies: « Extremely well. » So I also say that « She
is well. »
Our Lady speaks to Ivanka and tells her all the problems of the
Church and of the world. She cannot reveal anything yet. The
Madonna asked Ivanka to consecrate herself to Our Lady for six

months. A consecration to Our Lady – I asked what exactly this meant; it can be said that Our Lady asks that all one's being is consecrated to Her, all one's time, all one's actions and to do this with love and according to the intentions of the Madonna. Ivanka did not say this to me. However, as the Madonna always asks Ivan's group each Wednesday to consecrate all things, even the smallest, to Her intentions, I think that Our Lady asks the same of Ivanka. Marija, Ivan and Jakov have normal apparitions without a specific task or duty like Vicka or Ivanka. They pray, they commend the pilgrims, they ask for the blessing of objects, they pray once again, and through Marija the Madonna gives messages every Thursday.

We have closed the small chapel also to the pilgrims. There are reasons for doing this: the first and foremost is in view of the visionaries spiritual life. They must be guided in their prayers and we have no time or space apart from this, from five to six in the evening, to prepare for the apparition.

I led a one day retreat with the visionaries in January and I explained many things, also regarding our faith, our prayers, because seeing Our Lady does not mean being in a school of theology or prayer. For them, this is an impulse. They must be guided like everybody else. They once told me that when the chapel is packed, when photographs are being taken as they are entering and during the apparitions, they sometimes feel extremely empty. I told them that this happens equally when we do not prepare ourselves for Holy Communion, when we receive and go away immediately. We discussed what was the wisest thing to do and have acted accordingly. The visionaries did not have any time of their own in which to pray. Sometimes people looked for them in the sacristy or at our house or at their homes and because of this their spiritual lives were really in danger.

It is useless watching unless one prays. I often say that Judas saw everything that Jesus did and he heard everything. What good was it? Another reason why we had the chapel closed was that Our Lady said that no photographs should be taken. But several times those who were in the chapel disobeyed and photographed, and I was not happy as Our Lady repeatedly said: « *Now we must pray, pray.* » Well then, let us try and pray.

Another reason was this: every day there were lots of people who wanted to enter. If I let thirty go in another thirty were disappointed or angry. People were looking around and knocking continuously during the Rosary. It was impossible to pray. We have prayed very hard to know what best to do. Our whole community was under pressure about this.

Our Lady also said once: « *I am close to everybody.* » She also said that walls did not exist for her. And now that we are all present in the church (a bit in silence, a Hail Mary, some singing and we remain in church) we will receive additional graces. In many ways it is better – not only for the visionaries but also for the prayers in church and so as not to get angry at the beginning of Mass. Besides, Our Lady has never appeared in the chapel twice on the same day. And this is also a proof for me.

Yesterday Our Lady was with us for eight minutes: an enormous grace.

In Her message of February 14, She said: « *The family must pray together and read the Bible.* » I do not know many messages where Our Lady says « must. » Our Lady always offers all with love, She invites. Yet this is what She said in Her message. Then She added: « *I have spoken a great deal, but you have not responded. I am telling you for the last time, you can renew yourselves during this Lent. Unless you do, I no longer wish to speak.* » This must be understood in this way: Our Lady offers herself as our Mother and She knocks and speaks, saying: if you do not open up I do not want to force you. I no longer wish to speak.

Through Jelena She then said: « *I am not speaking for my salvation. I am saved. I speak for you and I want you to be saved.* »

To-day I said to Jelena: « Look Jelena, it seems somewhat strange that Our Lady is speaking in such a negative way. » Jelena gave her impressions on this matter. She said it was difficult for Our Lady to reprimand but She is often forced to simply because we ask for it. Who is it that asks for a telling off? All those who do not want to listen. For example, if in a family a child will not listen to what he is told, after a while he will be scolded. Who is it then who wanted to be scolded, the mother or the child? The child.

This is the explanation that twelve year old Jelena gives on how we must interpret Our Lady's criticisms. She says that Our Lady waits and is forever patient and never loses her temper with us. Before Christmas, at the beginning of Advent, Our Lady said: « *You still do not know how to love. I am your mother and I have come to teach you to love.* » This should stir us far more than the warning of a catastrophe. The greatest catastrophe is that of not loving. Yet we sometimes behave like little children who only react to warnings: it is better to react to love and to an invitation.

Through Ivan, Our Lady guides a prayer group and since the beginning of Lent She has been asking for many prayers and above all for meditation on His Passion until the 10th March, and from then till the 31st March to meditate on the sacred wounds, particularly on the sacred wound of His heart which is the most painful. Seven days before Easter, for Holy Week, She will tell us something else. She has said that we are to keep the Cross in mind. Jelena told me this morning that Our Lady has suggested how we should make the Stations of the Cross; by praying fervently and by meditating. And then She said we ought to carry objects which can help us live this passion more deeply. For example, She suggested carrying, not only a cross, but also the nails and some vinegar. Or even a sheet, a crown of thorns. In other words, all the symbols that can help to stimulate our faith.

(Fr. Slavko Barbarić - 25th February, 1985)

« To day is the Feast of the Mother of goodness, love and mercy », and She gave us her blessing

I meet two types of pilgrims – those who want to hear the news, and the arguments for and against; others who wish to move on and understand the messages more deeply.

We could really start off by dividing the pilgrims into those who want news and those who want to delve deeper.

It seems to me to be a waste of time to speak of the news and of the arguments for those who have already come and declared that they have felt faith within them. It really means wasting time and moving continuously backwards.

If I have discovered God along my path I have nothing to contest. If I am established on my path, if I have discovered a deeper meaning of the Gospel and the Gospel means something to me, I feel closer to God, so I have nothing to call in question. All I have to do is to go quickly forward in deepening my spiritual life.

Lately, following Our Lady's messages, we have seen that people do not know the meaning of the messages. People from far away know the messages – peace, prayer, fasting, sacramental life – but they do not really know what peace means, they are not able to follow the right path.

This is why I wish to remind you of some of the messages. I cannot remember the exact words by heart, but I remember their content and can stress the points which Our Lady spoke to us about.

I asked a question at the beginning of Lent to be able to set myself a pattern for Lent and lead the group. I was speaking about fasting and penance and I got an indirect reply. Our Lady said: *« Live honestly, sincerely, in humility and love. This road leads to me. »* You must understand this aspect of penance, the interior aspect, if you wish to find the spirit of Our Lady: humility, love, sincerity and prayer. And if you wish to understand the messages in depth move along this path; humility, sincerity, honesty, love of our neighbour, love of God, these are the fundamental attitudes. If you wish to go deeper into these aspects, these attitudes, then it is necessary to live an interior silence. Without interior silence you cannot go deeper into these aspects.

So we have discovered that interior silence is necessary to move forward in our spiritual life – silence will make us keenly sensitive to these messages and discover them even in our innermost feelings, in our thoughts; so that we may find interior freedom and feel humble, find love and be completely free.

As we move along this path, this silence moves along with us and draws closer to us.

This is why Our Lady is forever guiding us to discover this silence and feel in it complete liberty of prayer and action, where satan is not allowed to enter.

When Our Lady was speaking to us of satan's temptations (She spoke of them for one and half months), She warned us of the strong temptations and trials to which certain people, even the whole Parish, were exposed. However, She gave us the weapons to fight with, saying: fervent prayer, humility and love of our neighbour will not permit satan to come anywhere near us.

So this is the way of preventing temptations and it is very important. If you walk along this path towards depth you will continuously be discovering new shades of humility, of sincerity and of these fundamental attitudes, and in this way satan cannot come near you; he is unable to do anything; all he can do is to linger around as he lingered around Jesus Christ. But Jesus sent him away: go away, I live in another sphere where you cannot enter.

Jesus Christ's attitude during His trials shows us the way to live through Lent in our hearts. Jesus loved God beyond his daily bread because He lived according to the Divine Word. So for Jesus to live in God is far more important than to eat bread after fasting for forty days. Can you see how strong He was, how united He was to God!

During other temptations satan invited Him to jump off the Temple, just for fun. Jesus does not accept because He feels confirmed in God, He enjoys God, so no other forms of entertainment are necessary for Him.

The third temptation: all men wish to become powerful and strong, but Jesus does not. He obeys only the Father and submits Himself to the Father, even when satan offers Him the whole world. He does not accept anything. Can you see how united Jesus is to God.

When a person is united to God satan cannot do anything.

We have an example of this right here in Medjugorje to confirm what Our Lady told us: – One day Our Lady said to a small prayer group:* «*Follow my message tomorrow. Accept everything that happens tomorrow with love. All the obstacles. Accept everything with love so that tomorrow may be the day of Love.*»

So they all tried to put Her words into practice and to do everything with love: to study, to work, to overcome difficulties. And when evening came Our Lady appeared to Jelena and smiling, said: «*Dear children, You cannot imagine how satan flew from you to-day.*»

When we are in a complete state of grace, when we love – and it is impossible to love without humility, sincerity and honesty – when we live this way, then satan cannot draw anywhere near us.

In order to progress in our spiritual life, it is necessary to enter into a very subtle silence, thus discovering how to proceed during the day and at night, to discover at what point we have stopped.

What has greatly struck me deep in my heart, in these last few weeks, is Our Lady's blessing.

I particularly remember well the blessing given on the 29th December, 1984. It was the anniversary of the apparitions to Jelena. We had not realised this, but Our Lady told us to recite the prayer to Our Mother of Goodness, Mercy and Love, with very special devotion. In the evening She said: «*To-day is the feast of the Mother of Goodness, Mercy and Love*» and She gave us Her blessing. She then added: «*So far I have never given it to any-body,*» and I know that the whole group felt radically changed.

* The main prayer group is divided into several smaller groups.

I remember this very well. I had arrived tired and burdened with difficulties, but I returned home reassured.

I discovered how blessing and grace work.

Though afterwards, we discovered how easily we lose our graces.

While Our Lady was bestowing Her blessing on us, She said: «*Accept it, do not let go of it as before.*» We discovered it is easy to lose. It can be lost.

After a good confession we enter a state of deep spirituality and we must prolong this, continue it. And yet, after hardly a day, we realise we are once again on the wrong path. It is necessary to live inside our hearts. In a message delivered through Jelena, She said: «*I can give you my blessing, but I cannot give it to you unless you want it.*» So I understood that we can receive Grace, God is willing to give it to us if we are willing to accept it and to carry it within us, living in grace and practising it.

We must accept it with joy expressed through thanksgiving: where can I place this wonderous gift? What can I do with this money? It is a project worth thinking about.

So when we receive a grace, or a blessing, we must accept it as we would a precious pearl, protecting it and safeguarding it as an investment. This is the way we should accept a grace.

If we are ready to accept it in this way, then it will be plentiful because God is bounteous.

At the beginning of Lent I was asking several questions and the answers came in a message delivered through Jelena: «*Love one another. Love one another. Jesus easily moves people if you love one another.*»

Then we were given a message which particularly struck me. We have innumerable problems here in Medjugorje, many contentions are raised regarding this Parish and many of the arguments brought forward are hardly convincing. Our Lady said to us: «*At this moment I am present in every family because I love you. Do likewise and the world will be changed.*»

So the explanation is simple: the world can change only through love and not through arguments.

Our Lady said: «*I am present in every family,*» likewise we can be present in every person, in every living creature if we love and if we open our hearts entirely to God.

So you can see how we can influence every living person, we can change.

We may not be able to reach a high-ranking person in the Church to argue with him, but we can love. This is very important.

Nobody can tell you in so many words what you have to do.

You must discover this in your soul, within your group. You must exchange your experiences with the members of your group, feel these experiences in your heart as you pray.

A strong element which I felt last Saturday while Our Lady was explaining to the group how we ought to live the Sorrowful Mysteries during Lent was this: meditation.

Meditation in the sense that I must discover within me a path which I must follow.

So I understood: in the measure that I am able to reflect in my prayers, praying every day the Our Father, the Hail Mary, with new fervour, a new meditation, so I am proceeding forward.

If I do not discover these aspects in prayer I cannot proceed spiritually: my « Our Father » is at a standstill. It is valid, but I do not move forward. I do not deepen my spiritual life.

So through our prayer we must reflect. I hope you have understood that you cannot recite the Rosary without contemplating the mysteries – this internal contemplation is better than our prayer – our spiritual intention is better.

(Fr. Tomislav Vlašić - 2nd March, 1985)

« Pray so that all the trials which come from satan might result in the glory of God »

Our Lady still appears every day to all the visionaries.

The position of the visionaries is as follows: every evening She still tells Ivanka the problems facing the Church and the world, but Ivanka cannot reveal anything.

Our Lady has asked Ivanka to consecrate herself to Her for six months. Ivanka cannot reveal anything to me, but I have asked her: « What does this request mean to you? » She replied: « To consecrate everything to Our Lady for six months. »

She asked the group that prays with Ivanka to consecrate a day to Her: Wednesday. She said: « *Consecrate even the smallest things to me, to my mission.* »

Our Lady is telling Vicka the story of Her life in Nazareth, but she cannot say anything yet, she is writing it all down and one day it can be given for publication. We are waiting for this day but we do not know when it will be. The day is not important. What is important is that one day we shall be able to know about the life of Our Lady.

Jacov, Marija and Ivan pray with Our Lady and always commend all the sick and the pilgrims to Her.

The general message is this: Our Lady is with us. This is what is most important as every Thursday Our Lady has a message for us. She started last year in Lent and She wanted Thursday to become the day of the Parish. So She gives a message only once a week and often people ask: « What did Our Lady say? » I reply: « She has not said anything, » because the visionaries can only give us the message on Thursdays. So I say that Our Lady speaks to us on one particular day, but every day the message is there because Our Lady comes – She is with us.

One more thing. Our Lady asks for peace, for prayer, for fasting, for monthly confession, in order to be able to draw closer to Jesus. In this way all the other messages receive a special force from this general message: « *Our Lady is with us.* »

And this is the new spirit of prayer, the new spirit of penance, also the new spirit of love and reconciliation. The content of the messages before Christmas, during Advent, can be summarised in these words: « *You still do not know how to love. I am your Mother. I have come to teach you love.* » A programme to last us a lifetime.

I believe that these words should strike us and impress us, and we might ask: what do we react to more? When She says that we still do not know how to love, or when She says that catastrophes will take place? If we are more easily alarmed when we hear that catastrophes will occur then we are still on a level of a two, three or four year old child, when a mother says things like that to him. We mature Christians should react otherwise and move swiftly to the invitation: « You still do not know how to love. » This is the greatest criticism of our behavior if we do « not know how to love, » because through love everything becomes a treasure for paradise and for others. Without love all is destroyed.

Without love prayer has no value. Everything is worthless. So it is vital for us to learn to love: for us personally, for others and for God.

In Her last message Our Lady said: « *Dear children, I invite you to live these words this coming week: "I love God." Dear children, through love you will receive everything, even the things which seem impossible to you. The Lord wants you to belong to Him entirely: I wish it too.* »

You see, Our Lady is a mother who loves everybody, and every action, every word, everything we do must be with this in mind — « I love God. » And I say, every evening examine your consciences and ask yourselves whether your actions of the day have been true to this. So, we may say that the message of the fourth year is this: love.

Allow yourselves to be taught and learn how to love.

After Christmas, throughout January, She spoke a good deal about satan. She said: « *He attacks, he gets angry, he wants to destroy everything.* » Lately, in a message which spoke of satan She said: « *There is no need to be afraid of satan for it is easy to disarm him with ardent prayer and love.* »

These two things disarm satan.

She said another very important thing: « *Pray so that all the projects that come from satan might serve to the glory of the Lord.* »

So here is a great opportunity for us all: to act so that satan's plans might result in the glory of the Lord.

In February we had many difficulties, and might I tell you they are not over. They still recur and, we who are here say that they are in reality providential. We must learn how to love before we are faced with other trials. The Queen of Peace is a work of God: She cannot follow another path save the path of Jesus Christ. It would be false if we, like the Pharisees, were expecting a triumph, when instead, they were scandalized by Jesus' death on the Cross. What I mean to say is: every difficulty is in reality a difficulty, but also a grace for us. It is not easy, but it is a grace: something a little difficult for us all, but it is so.

Let me, for example, tell you this: when you return you will read about other attacks but, remember, without problems there is no progress. It is sad that it is so, but so it is and we must not worry. I say to you: be careful and do not discuss those who attack us or you will be near passing judgement on them. Quite frankly I must admit, that for me, it is not important whether a decree will establish or not that the apparitions are authentic, nor how the apparition takes place. If we pray, these things are not important. We have Lourdes that has been approved, we have Fatima that has been approved, we have the Gospels that have been approved: the Gospels are approved and what have we become socially? Therefore, Our Lady has not come to cause controversy or to discuss the issue on the apparitions – She has come to invite us.

So I ask you: Do not be carried away by arguments: just pray. Our Lady desires this from me, too. If we start arguing, if we get angry, then we will only start judging and Our Lady has not come for this.

I want to invite you to prayer, particularly next week, because there is another meeting of the Commission. What they will do, I do not know. I believe that Our Lady guides everything. I am not afraid because I have decided to follow Jesus, even before the apparitions began. One follows Jesus through difficulties and problems, so that when one comes here, one must look for faith: the same faith as Abraham, as in the introduction of the Mass. Abraham's faith which sees beyond what human eyes can see: taking his son, leading him to a hilltop and wanting to sacrifice him. It sounds crazy, but seen through the eyes of faith it is a different matter: it is an act of obedience which becomes salvation. It is with such a faith that we must pray. For us men it is crazy to accept the Cross, but in the eyes of Jesus, in the life of Jesus, it is something different: it is wisdom that comes from God. So our faith does not take us away from the world, from difficulties, or from problems, but it helps us to go on like a light in the darkness. Let us go forward like Abraham: pray in this sense that our faith may become more than human reasoning. I see many who say: I believe! Could they say: « I reason and my mind sees all? » This is not possible. Pray so that this faith might become something more than reasoning, more than mathematics with God.

Abraham is an example of how we ought to behave: to allow ourselves to be guided and see a little further when we meet difficulties, when we meet a cross, when we are ill...

Without this faith which sees a little further, the whole world would be grim; we would all be crazy had this faith not existed.

It is for this that fasting and prayer help to purify us and to increase our faith.

(Fr. Slavko Barbarić - 2nd March, 1985)

We must enter into our prayer before we begin to pray

I can say very little about Medjugorje at the moment. Father Slavko will give you more exact information.

I can give you some reflections and tell you what I have felt. It is difficult to speak to you now, to the people who have come here for the first time and to those who want to understand deeply. Most of the pilgrims and most of those who have come to Medjugorje know the messages: peace, conversion, fasting, sacramental life. But all this is nothing but words unless one knows the way that leads to it all. I can say that few, very few, know the messages that will lead us to a deep understanding. Only those who live close to Medjugorje, really close in spirit, can follow the messages. This is why I said to the pilgrims: we live in peace at Medjugorje while the people around Medjugorje are discussing the events. What characterizes the present moment is a progression on a hierarchal-ecclesiastical level on one side, and on a deeper one on the other.

You know what is happening at a hierarchal level, I am sure you know better than I do. You know the facts. There is no need to repeat them. I would like to stress only what is happening at a spiritual level. At least what I have experienced.

To begin with, we have experienced the presence of the evil one. For two months we were warned by Our Lady of the works of satan. Right at the beginning of the year She told us « *satan works under cover. Be careful* » and then She gave us the necessary means to overcome him and drive him away. In this way, before each trial, She warned us and told us something.

This experience was not only mental, we really have encountered satan as a living proof, a present being. And in this way several people have been upset and tempted. Some people, for example, have felt a strong urge to spit and to curse Jesus before drawing close to the Sacraments.

Several people have been physically attacked and tried.

I am speaking of this because I have had some trials too, of which I can testify personally. It was the experience of an encounter with satan who acts on the spot to prevent you from doing your work. For us here, these temptations are a positive fact, because they show that satan is upset and wants to attack.

According to me, as we go deeper in the Church, along the path of conversion, these temptations are stronger.

However the people who are walking along this path are also stronger to overcome him.

We have received concrete messages regarding this matter as to how to take a stand in front of satan. Once Our Lady told us: *« Fervent prayer, humility and love of your neighbour, will not allow satan to come near you. »*

So, if you live your prayers deeply, with humility and with love, satan cannot even come near you.

In this message Our Lady tells us how we ought to act and shows us the road that will lead us to peace.

At the beginning of Lent I liked the message. I asked several questions. Among these was the question on fasting. But the answer was different. Our Lady answered more or less like this: *« Honesty, love, humility and sincerity will bring you to me. »*

As you see She stressed the interior value of spiritual life and also of fasting.

When I asked a question regarding the numerous discussions and things written about Medjugorje: what shall we do? She always repeated: *« Look, now I am in every family, in every house. I am everywhere because I love. Do likewise. The world lives on love. »*

So you see, when we go down to the level of love and do everything with love, we can move every person beyond what scholars can do, but they too can be moved by this love lived by simple folk.

So you see that along this path which Our Lady follows, in particular with the Parish and with the prayer groups, these messages become a reality in people.

And along the path of the group we have discovered the depth of these messages. As we move along in our spiritual life subtle messages are given which can be understood only if there is profound silence and profound peace.

To help you along this path I will tell you what Our Lady told us in the group last Saturday.

She made us repeat a hymn three times. She told us « *Excuse me for making you repeat but I want you to sing with your hearts. Really you should do everything with your hearts.* »

And afterwards She taught us, She made us understand that at the beginning of each prayer people must be ready to pray. Many people pray a great deal but are always at the beginning, they do not move forward. So in order to begin praying one must do everything that is possible: if there are sins, one must remove them otherwise it is impossible to pray.

If there are any worries one must hand them over to Jesus.

« *You should not worry about your sins when you pray; sins must be left behind* »: namely sins must be put away at the beginning of prayer. You must enter prayer without carrying any burdens, you must unload them so that you may enter your prayer.

As we recited the Rosary of Jesus Christ we recited several mysteries, while She taught us. At the end She interrupted us and said: « *Well done, now go and pray.* » For, it is clear... we can discover this message in our daily practice: we recite prayers, yet we are always at the beginning. There is no change. When prayer is over, we are still the same.

In a message at the beginning of Lent, on the first Saturday following Ash Wednesday, Our Lady said: « *Look, you can receive a grace in an instant, in a month, in ten years, it depends on you. I do not need one hundred, two hundred Our Fathers — it is better to pray just one, but to pray in order to find God.* »

These messages take us to the depths. She does not say that there is no need to pray a great deal, but She wants to stress the quality of prayer. And we really must enter our prayers before praying, we must enter in the spirit of any work before starting it.

I myself have seen how I cannot celebrate Mass without this preparation. I feel I cannot do it. And each day I realise that this preparation requires a great effort so that I can be with Jesus.

(Fr. Tomislav Vlašić - 9th March, 1985)

«But why do you pray? To be with God, to feel God inside yourselves»

First of all I greet you. Welcome. I always regret when I cannot meet the people, either individually or in a group. I have a real pang in my heart whenever the messages are given for the world but they are not given to the people.

By the way, I can tell you that at Medjugorje a lot of messages are given by the visionaries; particularly those messages aiming at our spiritual growth, given through Jelena and Marijana, but they are not conveyed to the world.

I am going to tell you something from my point of view, because you will hear from Fr. Slavko at Medjugorje the latest news. He follows the visionaries and all that is happening day by day. He is the one that can give you the news.

I am giving you my thought, first of all on what I can see is happening in Medjugorje.

I am considering not only Medjugorje, but also the pilgrims coming from far away and I have already noticed some problems.

One of the problems is the increasing number of books about Medjugorje by several authors. In my opinion there is a danger in this, because several productions of books are being edited. On the contrary we must go straight on the road of spiritual growth, not editing books, not writing, but becoming saints, living the messages and conveying living messages. Each one of us must be first of all a living message.

There is the danger of hurrying to try to write new books, but always more or less the same. By so doing many of them bring the movement born in Medjugorje to a certain superficiality and, I am afraid, to a loss of strength.

I have had experience of a lot of movements that faded away when they came to the surface, when they became concerned with superficial things. On the other hand, every movement which had a saint in its bosom progressed. We must therefore aim at living the dynamics of the messages.

I can see another danger: there are always people asking: « What is happening now? have the apparitions come to an end? what are we to do now? »

When we are at a standstill it is satan who has done his job. A Christian must never be at a standstill: if you want to understand this, read yesterday's Gospel where Jesus says: « I will not judge you but Moses will. »

On the other hand, if we have lived what the priest says, what the Holy Scriptures say, what the rules say, we are able to understand also what Our Lady is saying now. If we have not done this previous work, as Jesus says: « Moses will judge you. Moses is your judge before God's throne. »

Now look, we must always move on this level, when we move on this level we can judge things, because we do not move on a rational level only, but on the level of faith. Faith, like the interior light, lights up the heart, because for faith rational arguments are not sufficient.

We cannot understand why God allowed His Son to be crucified. We cannot understand how life can be in the desert and why the Jews grumbled against God. It is something natural.

God has His own way, but those who have had an open heart and the interior light have followed this way. Who can understand by reason that a Virgin may conceive without a husband? This cannot be explained on a rational level, but on a level of faith. If we try to be enlightened on the level of faith, if this light increases within, we are always able to walk, to go on.

If we read that passage in the second epistle by St. Peter (first chapter) we can see how St. Peter progresses and how we must advance. First of all, he says, you must be honest, then join the knowledge of faith, then develop piety. In this way you will not be left, he says, neither without love nor without knowledge. So, if we progress by doing everything we have to do, the messages become clear and we are able to understand things.

With regard to Medjugorje I will only tell you certain things that are important for me, so that you may enter into the atmosphere of Medjugorje. Yesterday two men came who every now and then come to Medjugorje, and say: «I go to Medjugorje, because I come back a new man. I do not know how, but I feel happy when I am there.» And the other one says: «There, priests preach like nowhere else.»

Now, this does not mean that priests are cleverer there, but that there is a special grace. And this grace can be accepted, received only on the level of faith, not so much by introducing several rational subjects, but by practising faith, true confession, true communion, true prayer.

If we enter prayer in the religious sense, in the sense of faith, we can receive these messages like a special grace. The characteristic of the apparitions in Medjugorje now, is that the apparitions are still going on through the visionaries.

I have no news about Mirjana, about what happened on March 18 for her birthday. I only know that she had an apparition on Christmas Day 1984, but we have not seen her since.

All the other visionaries have apparitions every day. The essential point is that Our Lady, with Her messages, is driving the Parish forward and the world as well; She is always calling to conversion. At this level of Her call, it is very important to observe what Our Lady is saying through Jelena, because She gives the messages to the prayer group, messages for a spiritual growth, through her.

Maybe you will be a bit upset by what I am going to tell you: a week ago when I was in the prayer group, Our Lady asked us to meet three times a week during Lent. When we met, She said: «*This evening you are not going to say the Rosary. You must start again from the first class in school.*»

We, therefore, started with the first class on prayer. She taught us to pray the Our Father, and to practise only the Our Father. The first time, we spent an hour praying only the Our Father. Then She asked: «*But why are you praying? To be with God, to ex-*

perience God within. After five minutes for prayer something ought to happen within, if you do it properly. »

So we began to live every word and then we exchanged some ideas. After a week we thought it over and somebody said: « I have been trying by myself for the last month, but I had great difficulty in uttering the words forgive us our trespasses, as we forgive those who trespass against us. I began then saying aloud in my room: "I forgive that person." But I could not physically utter these words. I had to practice for a whole month to be able to forgive and to be able to live this part of the prayer. Then when I started saying: "Thy will be done," I felt it was so difficult to utter, in every situation, "Thy will be done." »

Well, you can see what we are doing: we are not doing anything new, but Our Lady wants to lead us to the depth of prayer, to the depth of life.

At the beginning of Lent She said: « *But you can receive a grace in an instant, in ten days, in ten years, in one hundred years. It is up to you, to the intentions of your heart.* »

Just now it is clearly noticeable that Our Lady wants to lead us to meet the living God in our prayer. And through this encounter to be able to live, truly live.

We have discovered that many Christians say their prayers, say a lot of prayers and they do not know what they want.

After this exercise we had three other meetings. During every one Our Lady emphasized this exercise of the Our Father, and once She said: « *You should understand, the Our Father ought to be like a continuous melody for you.* »

We should feel as children of an almightly and great Father, in order to be able to live this reality.

Now I have not told you everything. I have told you what Our Lady taught us in order to practise, to exercise the Our Father. But when you are made to exercise a prayer in this way, your eyes open just as the Apostles' eyes were opened after the Resurrection.

For instance, for us priests, the problem of how to preach is typical. Since I have been doing this exercise I have not had this problem. With the Scriptures your eyes open. With the text of Exodus and

Numbers, when they deal with the Alliance, when God, so to speak, was cross with the people; do you know what happened? He wanted to destroy the people and He said to Moses: « I am going to make a new people from you. » Moses prays, but do you know how he prays? He does not say a prayer, he does not say some prayers by heart; instead he enters into God's very heart. And so to speak, he makes God charge his mind...

As when we see a person in a mood we say: why are you in a mood? Come, consider this or that...

So Moses entered into God's heart and said: « You are good, remember the past, your promises, your goodness. »

He made Him rise again, he made Him change His mind. Look at the depth of renunciation on the part of Moses. Those people were also troublesome to him. But when God said He wanted to destroy them, Moses said: « No, not that. I want the conversion of the sinners. » So you see what praying means: it means renouncing all, renouncing and living for your fellow men, going every time we pray, into God's heart. Driving away the wrath, making that positive part of the divine heart flourish again, discharging it of anger, to make what is positive rise again, then we pray. This is then prayer.

Now we must live this. When Our Lady says: « *pray, pray* », we have not only to say our prayers by heart, but feel the sinners around us and pray, beg, remember all the divine promises, all Our Lady's promises, remember all the tears, all the martyrs. Inside, we must be a new person.

First of all we have to go on being, like Moses, always good and not like the others who became unfaithful. If we want to carry on the messages, we must continue being good in every situation, even in a very very bad one.

We must be capable of awakening the divine heart.

(Fr. Tomislav Vlašić - 22nd March, 1985)

« I am beautiful because I love. If you want to be beautiful, love »

I am going to explain to you, a bit, the position of the visionaries: All five visionaries still have the apparitions. Marijana had these apparitions on her birthday; I spoke to her last Sunday, 17, on the day before her birthday: she said that at Christmas she had half an hour's apparition and Our Lady said She would speak to her but would not show herself. She told me that Our Lady had spoken to her at the end of February and also last Sunday for maybe twenty minutes, about atheists, unbelievers and concerning the secrets and she had prayed with Her for these intentions. And on this day, February 28, Our Lady promised she would appear to her twice: on her birthday and on the feast of St. Joseph, that is on the day after. So on the following day, Wednesday, I rang her up and she told me she had had the apparitions, but she could not tell me more over the 'phone. She cannot reveal the details or any further information yet. Anyway, we can say that Mirjana has a special duty towards unbelievers and Our Lady always asks her to pray a lot for atheists, for unbelievers.

Our Lady is still telling Vicka the story of Her life. Vicka writes everything down but it cannot be checked because Our Lady asked her not to show it to anybody until she has finished everything. Also, Our Lady is telling Ivanka the problems of the Church and of the world, but nothing can be revealed yet. Marija, Ivan and Jacov pray with Our Lady and She gives the messages through Marija. Now I am going to say something about Vicka's health: when you ask her how she is, she says « fine ». But this must be understood as meaning: Vicka is ill, but she bears her suffering and illness with total abandonment and even with joy. And this I believe is a very important message for us all. The visionaries have their own sufferings and they bear them; for instance Vicka lets none of the other visionaries ask Our Lady about her health, instead she accepts her condition and is resigned to it. Bishop Franić told me once, that in his opinion, a great standard of genuineness of the apparitions can be measured by how the visionaries speak of their sufferings, as they would about health, because only Our Lord can carry a person near the Cross or to the Cross with love, patience and joy.

Vicka has got a cyst between her brain and cerebellum and with the changing of the weather she falls into a state which prevents her from communicating with anybody, even for three, four or ten hours. Vicka is convinced that all this has been sent by Our Lady and therefore I am sure Vicka has accepted the suffering from Our Lady, but nobody knows the reason and she does not want to reveal it.

At the end of January (31st January) Our Lady gave a message in which She asked us all to open ourselves to God as flowers do in the springtime, to long for Our Lord as flowers long for the sun. On 21st February She said: «*Dear children, day after day I am inviting you to pray, to renew your lives, but if you are not willing to follow me, I am not going to give any more messages. But during this Lent you can be renewed. I am inviting you.*» This was the message at the beginning of Lent.

I myself was a little afraid. I said to myself: if Our Lady is not going to speak any more, to give any further messages, it will be very sad. On the following Thursday (28th February) She spoke and gave a most beautiful message: «*Dear children, I am inviting you to live the words: "I love God." Dear children, by loving you can receive anything, even things that seem impossible to you. Our Lord wants you to belong to Him entirely, and so do I. I thank you because you have responded to my call.*» On Thursday (14th March) She said: «*Dear children, you all have experienced evil and good, light and darkness in your lives. Our Lord gives the power and the strength of discerning good from evil; I invite you to the light which you should bring to all who are in darkness. Day by day, many people who are in darkness come to you. Dear children, give them light.*»

Yesterday (21st March) She gave this message: *« I am going to give you my messages also in future and therefore, for this reason, I invite you: accept and live my messages. Dear children, I love you. This Parish which I have chosen in a special way is very dear to me, dearer than all the other places where I have appeared or where Our Lord sent me. Therefore, listen and accept my messages. Again I thank you for listening to my call. »*

Our Lady speaks in this way, giving short messages like impulses and these messages are always like a school... Our Lady wants to teach us and She gives us a message every Thursday. However, she speaks to the visionaries every evening, but from our point of view there is nothing special with regard to words. Every apparition is a great message, which is: *« I am with you. »* When She shows herself to the visionaries, the message for us all is: *« I am with you. »* One day a group came, I do not know from where; there were about twenty-five children. I invited Marija to speak to them a little and I said to the grown-ups: « please be silent so that the little ones can ask questions. » They were very interesting questions. A child asked: « Does Our Lady come when it rains? » Marija replied: « Yes, of course She comes. » « So is She wet when it rains? » Marija laughed and said: « No, no She is not. » And I added: « Our Lady does not only come when it is sunny in our hearts, but even when it is raining, even when we are in trouble. We are the ones who sometimes come only when it is sunny. Our Lady is always with us. Do not wait for the rain, but be always with Our Lady. »

Every time Our Lady appears there is a message. And this is a reason you can call theological, pedagogical-educational.

Why do so many people feel a little annoyed? Why has Our Lady been appearing for such a long time? I say I would never have ventured to hope for a situation like this. Impossible. And the day after tomorrow it will be forty-five months since the visionaries first saw Our Lady. Most people believe and accept. Just a few say they are hallucinations. Then they say that it is perhaps some other kind of illness, but they refuse to see this, they cannot see all that is happening.

And the visionaries have been through a lot of difficult situations. They always say: « We are with Our Lady, we can see Our Lady. » When somebody asks why is She appearing for such a long time? I say I do not know. But I am sure it is real.

Maybe you have heard that some doctors from France together with Laurentin made some further experiments at the end of December; for instance, on their sight and it can be said that manipulation, hallucination or suggestion are absolutely impossible. The reaction comes at a fifth of a second and this cannot be explained unless we accept the facts as the visionaries explain it: « When we begin to pray we can see a light and we kneel down. » I would say that this goes beyond science; it is incapable of explaining it. They say it is inexplicable. Then faith has to look for an answer. You must always jump to faith. I spoke to a German, who said to me: « I did not come to see anything and I do not care what happens with the visionaries. Just the fact that something like this is possible has appealed to me strongly, I am living a new life. » A month ago Our Lady appeared to little Jelena who asked Her: « My Lady, why are you so beautiful? » The answer was: « *I am beautiful because I love. If you want to become beautiful, love and you will not need the mirror so much.* » So, Our Lady speaks on a child's level.

I say: look, we all have got a chance to become beautiful in our lives if there is love. This works for us all, either as our greatest chance or our greatest judgement. If Our Lady says: « *You do not know how to love yet,* » this is the very thing we should be upset about. All the world's problems and those in our lives come because we do not know how to love, not because we have not got as much money as we need or anything of the sort. Problems come when we do not love. Love is another word for conversion. Nobody can say « I was converted yesterday. » Conversion is a process and nobody can say « I loved yesterday. » A child is not interested in yesterday, he wants to be loved by his mother, to-day.

This is a very important thing, therefore, when Our Lady invites us to prayer, fasting and love.

(Fr. Slavko Barbarić - 22nd March, 1985)

« Be reconciled with Our Lord »

... I would like you to be conscious again to-day of Our Lady being close to you like a mother helping us to say our « yes » with all our heart, as She said in yesterday's message (22rd March): « *You cannot belong to Our Lord entirely and you cannot live this feast fully if you are not reconciled.* »

Let us be reconciled with Our Lord and with our fellow men so that we may celebrate to-day's feast.

It was forty-five months yesterday evening since Our Lady first appeared to the visionaries. And to-day it is forty-five months since She began speaking to them. An unbelievable story during these months.

While seeing and living a little this story, in this situation, I can now say that I understand what believing in God really means, what listening to Our Lord's Word means, what it means when Our Lady says: « *Abandon yourselves to Our Lord* »; what it means « to be reconciled, » but also what it means when we are all very far from God. When you start along the path of peace, of radical love, you can understand what Our Lady once said: « *You do not know yet how to love.* »

And this is the same thing we discover here and it is also a motivation to go in a deeper and more radical way with Our Blessed Virgin.

I am now going to say something about yesterday evening's message...

Our Lady usually speaks every Thursday, but sometimes She gives Her messages on another day. Yesterday I was present at the time of the apparition; only Marija and Jacov were there. Ivan had gone to Makarska for an exam and had not yet returned. Vicka is ill. Ivanka was at home.

These two were in the presbytery. I prayed with them. The apparition lasted almost three minutes. After the apparition they write all that they had seen or all that happened in a copybook.

Marija needed ten minutes to write everything down and said to me: « This evening there is a message. » And this message contains all that Our Lady has been saying during these months. She said: « *To-day I am inviting you to confession even if you have been only a few days ago. I would like you to be able to live my feast in your hearts. But you cannot live it if you do not abandon yourselves wholly to Our Lord. I am inviting you, therefore, to be reconciled to the Lord.* »

At the beginning of these forty-five months the first words were: « Pray, be converted, recite the Creed and seven Our Father's. » Now you can see all praying, all prayers and fasting as an invitation to be reconciled to Our Lord.

Being reconciled to Our Lord, therefore, means renewing our state of mind, changing our lives and that of all mankind. You know that the first sin was disobedience to Our Lord. Man became alienated from God and the whole of creation was against man.

Being reconciled to Our Lord in the core of our souls, in our hearts, means finding Paradise again. And how can we find Paradise again? What is the meaning of reconciliation with God?

The first thing is this; let yourselves be guided by the Lord, be trusting.

Man's first sin was this; not to trust in God and to think, if I do something different to what Our Lord tells me, I will be happy. Trusting in the Lord means to let ourselves be guided and to believe in His Word, to believe that the road Our Lord leads us along is the safest for man and for all mankind. And when one puts one's trust in the Lord, then peace can grow, this abandonment can grow, love can also grow.

Being reconciled in God then means also accepting the plan of my life which the Almighty Father has planned for me, the plan Our Lady wants us to discover. Our problem is always that we want to live our own lives, our own plans and sometimes, more often than not, outside Our Lord's plans.

Therefore, letting myself be guided and having trust in Our Lord means accepting the plan of my life coming from Our Lord, but discovered in my heart. For this reason again we must fast and pray.

Fasting purifies us in the depths of our souls and of our hearts and in this way we can discover the love of Our Lord for us.

In this way also the sick discover that this is the path for the acceptance of God's will. They discover that even in suffering the Lord leads us and is not far from us; even in suffering problems make sense. Without this trust in Our Lord, without praying and fasting you cannot see and you cannot accept this wonderful plan Our Lord has in mind for us.

If we want to see Our Lady's life in the light of to-day's feast, we can say that Our Lady, as a girl of the chosen people, knew all God's promises and let herself be guided. We are all certain that She did not know on the day of the Annunciation that the day of Calvary would follow; She was not aware of the difficulties and problems, but this was not important. Our Lady had prepared Herself and was ready at the moment of the Annunciation to accept the plan coming from beyond.

God's plan was for Her to become the Mother, the Virgin Mother. Her plan was, if I may say so, another one. But in her innermost self She was ready to accept this plan from God.

This is for me, the greatest feast: Our Lady prepared Herself for the Annunciation and when She said: « Yes », She had no idea what was in store for Her; something very different was in store for Her: even the nativity in Bethlehem, the death and the Resurrection. Our Blessed Virgin did not know this plan, but She went ahead step by step.

Reconciliation means this: accepting, saying: « yes », and going onward together with Our Lady.

These apparitions have been lasting for forty-five months. They are like a preparation. Our Lady wants to prepare us, She wants to educate us. You can express it in a theological thought: Our Lady is setting out with this Church, in this world, in these circumstances, on a new journey. She accompanies, invites and wants us all to become a real Church, believing in God, growing in love, peace and reconciliation.

With regard to prayer groups, I can say: Our Lady asks for prayer and we must pray either in groups, in our families or alone. From what we see with the prayer group She is leading with a certain method, through Jelena; She is asking for certain stages in prayer: for prayer alone, for prayer as a group and praying in couples.

She asks also for a third and fourth thing; for instance, it is a good thing to select someone in the group for a week, to meet each other, to pray a little together and then to discuss things over a cup of coffee; to be a little together so as to get to know each other. When members of a group are well acquainted, the group then grows, it can give mutual help.

Another thing is this: when you come together to pray, if in the group there is trouble, if something is bothering you, even a member of the group, then you must say so from the start, almost like a confession. Because, She explained, through Jelena, if you have not forgiven, if you have not said that a person is troubling you, you cannot love that person. And if you do not love, it means that you are self-centred, you are closed and others, therefore, cannot love you. This is the first step in prayer in the group.

The second one is this: reading the Word and saying what this means to me.

The third stage is seeking the blessing, which means praying.

When we are acquainted, when we know our difficulties, we can also pray together. But I must tell you that you have to be very patient with yourselves and with the others in your groups, in your communities and in your families in the same way as Our Lady is with us.

At first She asked for the Creed and seven Our Father's and then, step by step, She asked for a Rosary, then the whole Rosary and then a second day of fasting.

Therefore, if some of you cannot pray as Our Lady asks this does not mean you need not begin; if some of you cannot fast, this does not mean you need not begin.

Fasting and praying are part of Christian life and are means of reconciliation, of feeling what is happening in our hearts: they are an invitation to walk together with the Blessed Virgin.

(Fr. Slavko Barbarić - 25th March, 1985)

« In our daily lives, we must find the Word of God which saves us in a real way »

In order to follow the path of prayer in these two festivities which we have celebrated (St. Joseph and the Annunciation), Our Lady stresses the importance of two main points, to the prayer group: prayer in the morning and again in the evening.

Through morning prayer we enter the day and we all have experienced the fact that when we do not start by praying, by a morning meeting with God, we cannot truly live the day; it just slips by and we often live without God even if we are Catholics. It is very important to meet God in the morning. It is also useful to meet God in the evening: as we know that the evening is the preparation for the morning. A wonderful example of this was St. Joseph to whom God spoke in his dreams: he was God's representative to protect the Holy Family and he was in God. That was why God could speak to him even in dreams.

To people who watch television, television speaks in their dreams. To people who worry about material things, worries speak in dreams. But those who enter sleep with God live with God even in dreams.

Yesterday's festivity was just one particular morning; every morning we must awake as the Blessed Virgin was awakened by the Angel! Just as a flower does, She opened Herself to him and said: « Your will be done! » What we must do is to go on living every day like yesterday. In order to live it, however, we must look for God's Word in our daily life. Our Lady is said to be everywhere. It is true. But when She appears in a particular place it is a particular gift from God that we must receive.

The same is true for me: if I want to live the reality of salvation, every day, I must look for and receive the Word of salvation that saves me; if I am upset, I must find the Word that brings me peace; if I am ill I must seek the Word that relieves my illness, gives me peace, safety.

In this way, we see that in every day life, we must find God's Word that saves us in a practical way. If we go on practically every day, what we were told yesterday and the day before about living a deep confession, living it like a daily meeting with God, renewing it, then we will progress.

Our Lady's divine messages can never be stopped by anybody.

They can only spread.

Now it is my wish that, what we have been celebrating and what is written in the Gospel, what happened to the Blessed Virgin, may also happen to us every day; that even impossible things may become possible.

You will then discover that even the mountains can be moved, even death, when impossible things become possible.

But try to do it practically. When you feel surrounded by impossible problems, by troubles, meetings with God must always bring fruits of great joy, security and peace.

(Fr. Tomislav Vlašić - 26th March, 1985)

« I say to you: love »

People ask information about Medjugorje and its messages, but there is little to say. We usually give some explanations, some news, but Our Lady does not bring news: like a Mother, She awakens, incites, calls, rebukes... There is nothing new.

It is the same when She tells us to go deep into our inmost self.

In the moment when these messages are given one feels an interior opening, light comes. The words are the same, but the heart understands the depth.

On this plane, many messages are now being given and those listening to the messages are following an interior path.

It is very important to follow this interior path and open ourselves to the light.

By the way, for the last few weeks Our Lady has been teaching the prayer group how to live the Our Father. How to live every single word, how to really feel it within.

It is not a question of receiving news, but of going deeper into how we live day by day, in a new light.

Now that Medjugorje is under so much discussion I want to tell you what Our Lady said at the beginning of Lent, through the visionary Jelena: « *Look, now I am here. I am in every family. I am everywhere. It may seem strange to you, but it is not. This is what love does. I tell you: love.* »

You see, we must understand that love has its influence everywhere. We must move towards love, live love. Our strength is love, not human arguments; rather the strength of love together with human discussions. But all human arguments without love can do nothing and we must move towards the core of this message.

May you all live these days in Medjugorje with love and with a new light and may you take this light to others.

I suggest to the pilgrims that instead of taking photographs, recording and filming... you yourselves should become a videocassette, a recorder, for others!

(Fr. Tomislav Vlašić - 29th March, 1985)

« Pray with your hearts »

In a message of 28th March, Our Lady said: « *In prayer you will find the deepest joy.* » But precisely in that prayer is where you find Our Lord.

Prayer is a meeting with God speaking to us, leading us, giving us light, saving us. Our Lord who introduced himself as a Father and Jesus Christ as our brother, as our friend.

In our meeting with Him we must have a deeper joy and none of us has anything against this deep joy.

We must wonder how to pray, how to meet this Father, this brother, this friend?

God revealed Himself in Jesus Christ.

Before this, Our Lady also said another thing: « Pray with your hearts, » that is not only to repeat something in words.

An example: in a kitchen you can find every kind of food, but you can still starve if you do not eat well or if you do not eat at all.

Many people pray but do not feel this joy, this deep peace.

Why? We must say: they do not pray as they should, they do not meet Our Lord as they ought to in order to receive this joy. What may be their predicament to pray and not feel anything?

If you want to meet one of your friends, you must look for him, you must find time to speak to him, to listen to him...

If you want to have a satisfactory meeting you make preparations so that you will not be disturbed. If you do not have the time, if you do not try to arrange the meeting, if you do not try to say anything to the other person, you cannot have a meeting even on a human level.

And the same thing can be said, I think, also of prayer if you are determined to pray. At the beginning of Her apparitions, Our

Lady used to recommend: « recite the Creed. » If you have made up your minds to carry out whatever Our Lady has asked of you, you must get ready; that is, find the time and take time when you can be for God alone, when the telephone cannot interrupt you, nor your wife... a little corner in your house, and say: this half hour is only for prayer.

Find the time, the place and begin as you can.

I am telling you to begin as you can. In the beginning Our Lady requested: the Creed, seven Our Father's and fasting (one day of the week). They are the concrete and simple things to begin with. And anyone who has begun like this, finding every day a little time for prayer, has been able to learn how to pray.

We must begin as when we started to pronounce the first words with our mothers. We must begin as we can and go on continuously in this way.

Look for a time, a place; try to speak to and listen to God. In this concrete manner it is possible to go deeply into prayer and you will, from day to day, feel a mood for prayer.

Do not just say: « I want to pray, » without following this method. The same thing is true if you say: « I want to be a doctor, » but you do not want to study. This is not taking things seriously... How can you hope to reach the goal if you do not wish to use the means to attain it? How can you want joy and deep peace and not the means to reach them? How can you want to pray if you do not pray? How can you want to meet the Lord if you do not try to fulfil these conditions?

One more thing – create a habit.

You say, the appetite grows by eating, and I say: also prayer grows by praying, and fasting grows by fasting.

Being unable to pray like St. Francis used to, does not mean I need not begin.

This is the journey Our Lady asks of us.

If you are absent-minded, you go to prayer with this absent-mindedness.

The first concrete start was very simply, to say seven Our Father's. In August last Our Lady asked for the whole Rosary.

The Rosary is a repetitive prayer, but also a rhythmic, meditative and biblical one.

You can recite it in your families, even with the children.

You may change something: a little silence, some singing, some words of praise, some spontaneous prayers and the repeating of Hail Mary, Hail Mary...

And I can say that if it should happen to you, as it did to St. Francis, to begin the Our Father and then continue all night long repeating only « Our Father », experiencing its sweetness in your mouth and in your heart, you will have all the same followed the Blessed Virgin, even though you may not have recited one Hail Mary.

It is not a matter of just saying: I have recited one hundred and fifty Hail Mary's.

You must begin to pray with your heart and you will learn this little by little, every day, step by step. If you have had a frustrating and weary day, of course, your prayer cannot be the same as on a day when you are not weary; your prayer must be according to your capabilities, according to where you have reached. Your prayer is the expression of your soul, where joy, love, reconciliation grow... But every day you must go on as best you can and in so doing you will reach joy and be able to pray with your heart, with an ever deeper joy.

Fasting is connected a great deal to prayer, but it has another function – to set us free from matter, from distressing anxieties. And fasting opens us, our body too, to the Word. The Word can better be incarnate, become flesh more easily in our bodies if we fast.

We all know what we must do (we do not need apparitions) – love.

Jesus said: « especially your neighbour, like yourself. »

Everybody wants peace: but it is not enough to know this.

If we begin fasting Our Lord can purify us step by step.

And this purification gives the possibility to the Word to become incarnate in our souls, in our sentiments. We are not yet open. By fasting, we get ready, step by step to say our « Yes », as Our

Lady did so that the word of love and of peace may become incarnate and take shape.

By fasting and praying we get nearer and nearer to Our Lord and so we get nearer to peace and to love: to what Our Lady has asked of us.

Our Lady has a lot of patience with us, so we must have patience with ourselves and with others. Some people have told me: now we find time more easily for the whole Rosary than we did at the beginning for the Creed and the seven Our Father's.

Our Lady leads us step by step and She also does not want us to force ourselves or others.

See what you can do to-day and go on. But always go on every day. Praying and fasting are the means to get ready, to accept the grace of peace, faith and love.

The aim of fasting and of prayer is not in fasting and prayer in itself. We do not pray to waste time, we do not fast to be hungry. These are only means for us, to meet Someone, to feel Him and to be able to receive the Word for ourselves.

(Fr. Slavko Barbarić - 30th March, 1985)

Our Father

Greetings and Welcome! I am always sorry when I have not got much time when pilgrims are coming.

You know, these days, we priests have many commitments and besides we also need to' pray instead of speaking to others. And sometimes our words become empty...

In Medjugorje, you will hear the latest information on what is happening.

I can only say that the apparitions are still continuing.

Also Mirjana, who lives in Sarajevo, has had several apparitions, besides the one on her birthday. We do not know any details about these because we have not seen her in these last few weeks.

The other visionaries continue having the apparitions.

Our Lady is telling Ivanka events of the future.

She seems to be at the end of telling Vicka the history of Her life and is giving messages through the other children. Messages more of an interior nature are being given through Jelena. They are very beautiful just because they lead the soul forward and explain how it must open up.

I am now going to dwell a little on these messages.

For almost three weeks we have been practising only the prayer of Our Father. Together with the Blessed Virgin the only work we do is really savouring every word there is in the Our Father.*

Our Lady is leading us to live every word and says: « *Better say and live one Our Father than say one hundred.* »

She really wants to lead us into prayer, so while praying the Our Father, we may feel free to be able to pray: « Our Father. »

* See the text translated from Croatian p. 218.

There is a long preparation for an Our Father. Our Lady has pointed out a mistake Christians make. She says: « *Many people go to pray without entering into prayer.* »

To enter into prayer you need to unburden yourself of all your sins, admit them before the community, the group.

Besides the confession, you need to acknowledge the sin before the person you have offended.

That is, to acknowledge one's foibles in the group, in the family. To acknowledge all that oppresses us, to unburden our sins and not to remember them any longer in prayer.

The pang of conscience cannot remain in prayer, it must be cast out.

The other step is giving all one's cares to Jesus and giving Him all our problems. In this way we are free. We can then enter into prayer and be with Him. Otherwise, Our Lady says: « *You always remain at the beginning of your prayer. You reach the initial step and you are always beginning your prayer from there.* »

Before praying it is important to always unload our sins, every sin. To acknowledge them and not only myself but I must express them outwardly, tell others I have offended them even in the face of those I am scared of. I must rid myself of everything in order to free myself. I must do the same also with worries so that they may come to the light of faith before the community.

Only then can I begin to pray, and this is no easy task.

Someone told me it took him a week to say only physically: « I forgive you. » He could not physically utter: « I forgive you. » And he said: « I saw I could not pray: "Our Father, forgive us our trespasses". »

So you see, if you try to live in your life and in your attitude every word of the Our Father and try to change and become free you will see that when you say the Our Father, every day it will take on a new meaning.

I remember that three days ago, only the second part of the Our Father came alive within me. I felt the need of crying « forgive us our wrongs » because I felt so many sins of the past within me and in the world. Forgive us, otherwise we cannot move forward.

« Forgive... lead us not into temptation... »

I felt inside me, I cannot move without God, He must take my hand so that I can go on walking. I felt a very deep need in me in the second part of the Our Father. So you see Our Lady wants to stir us to prayer in this sense in order to deepen our prayer and so enable us to continue with our traditional prayers on a new dimension. They are, however, no longer traditional.

The contents are new, because there is interior light. Now you do not need to look for a lot of prayers. Instead you need to express yourselves in the prayer that Our Lord taught us.

In this way the Rosary and the other prayers become new, according to the new light inside our hearts.

There is then another very important element, according to Our Lady, who said: « *When you have entered prayer you can then pray for God's plans.* » Because when God is inside us, He suggests these plans to us in prayer: we agree with Him if we are unburdened of sins, of cares. The Holy Spirit speaks to us within, tells us what we must do.

Eventually, when we are told, ask for a blessing. In this sense it is no magic.

It is something tangible. During prayer I have discovered inside myself what God wants of me. I have discovered what I am to do. Then I ask for strength.

But now I must cherish this pearl that I have discovered.

Then Our Lady said: « *Do not ask for blessings as you did last time. You asked for it but you did not keep hold of it.* »

Well, so you see that prayer must have an incentive, an introduction and must also have an end. At the same time we see that it must continue in life, because if we lose our pearl then our prayer is useless.

You can see that there is a certain continuation from prayer to life and from life to prayer. And if you go on praying like this, life changes but at the same time also our prayer changes.

So, during to-day and to-morrow I would like you to pay attention to this interior voice in order to go deeper into the Our Father.

And remember that, Our Lady, through Jelena, suggested and

begged that also to-morrow we fast and keep vigil up to one hour after midnight.

Then, after the liturgy, families usually go home to pray or gather in groups. People go on to the mountain or stay here in the church. Our Lady asked the parishioners to continue their vigil until one o'clock in the morning.

Pray much for the intentions of the Blessed Virgin as She has asked us to do of late; and so that this programme may go forward in the Church.

So best wishes for a happy Easter.

Pray a lot, especially for priests, monks, nuns who are in Medjugorje, that they may live and serve others because they really need to have greater strength than others in order to bear up and to be at everybodys' disposal.

Best wishes. I will be with you in prayer.

(Fr. Tomislav Vlašić - 5th April, 1985)

« I knock, but there are so many hearts that still do not open to Me »

Yesterday evening (Maundy Thursday) there was the following message: « *Dear children, I thank you because you have begun thinking more of Our Lord's glory in your hearts. Today is the day when I did not intend giving you the messages any longer because there are some of you who do not accept them. The parish has, however, moved. They have responded. And from now on I want to give you my messages in such a way as has never happened since the beginning of the world.* »

The first part of this message is very important: « *Dear children, I thank you because you have begun praying more in your hearts to Our Lord's glory.* »

When Our Lady gives such a message, when She says it in this way, an explanation is not difficult, but it is, all the same, very important to understand it.

During these days and especially on the feast of the Annunciation, on the one hand, we came across great difficulties and on the other, we experienced many graces.

Let us hope that these difficulties even inside ourselves, in our hearts, may undergo change, which once Our Lady spoke about in a message: « *Dear children, pray that all the trials coming from satan may end to Our Lord's glory.* » It seems to me that in this message a very important thing has become true; from these very difficulties a further advance towards Our Lord's glory is coming about.

Another thing; we thought that Our Lady would not give any further messages and I believe this to be due to the difficulties we happen to have.

Only Our Lord can find a solution to some of the things here, and through our prayers. In fact in the last message but one, Our Lady said: « *In prayer you will feel or find the solution even to the most difficult situations that seem impossible to you.* »

If Our Lady says something particular in this message, She also wants to bring to our attention every other message. The « message » is a new way that has never been seen before since the beginning of the world. Facing these events taking place among us for the last forty-five months we have been going on through incredible difficulties. Every evening there were a lot of people (even bishops and priests) asking: « is it possible for Our Lady to appear in this way? »

As far as I know I would never have thought Our Lady would appear every evening for such a long time. How can we account for this?

Prof. Joyeux explained that the visionaries, all together, react in a fifth of a second. An absolute synchronism impossible to be accounted for. They say: our reaction is towards the light coming before Our Lady, then we kneel. They see this light, but we do not. So the reaction actually is there. How to explain this? He says that scientifically it is inexplicable.

What can we do? Accept and believe and let these events move us. We have been living them for forty-five months in spite of all the difficulties. And you could say they continue moving the whole world.

Now I feel it is time to conclude this short account.

You know that Jesus said to John under the Cross: « Here is your Mother. » And to his Mother He said: « Here is your son. »

When John wrote the Apocalypse, he saw a woman who wore the sun for her mantle. I think this is the very thing that happens in these messages, every evening, when Our Lady comes, full of graces: « Here is your Mother. » « Here is your son. » Our Lady has taken seriously these words under the Cross and every Thursday, in every message, it is as if she said: « Dear children, this Cross is built according to Our Lord's providence (on Mount Krizevac): pray before that Cross. »

So today again who can understand those words if not we who hear them every evening: « *Dear children* »?

Yesterday I asked the visionaries how the apparition took place: Our Lady came and said « *Jesus Christ be praised,* » she prayed with us and we commended everybody to Her. We prayed for a blessing and finally She again said: « *Go in Our Lord's peace.* » What Our Lady tells the visionaries every evening is also for us: « *Jesus Christ be praised.* » He died for everybody and from the Cross He said to her: « look, this is your son. » We were all represented in John standing under the Cross with Our Lady. So who can understand these events but we who hear these words every evening? Who can accept Our Lady as our Mother but we and all those who have followed these events and you who will follow us with your prayers?

Together with Our Lady I ask you: « pray, pray, pray. »

Jesus defeated satan with His Cross but satan continues spoiling Our Lord's plans. In a message Our Lady said: « *Even if you fall in the trial, do not stop.* » So act and go forward.

I would like us all this evening to accept that « here is your Mother, » accept « here is your son. »

In a message Our Lady said: « *I knock, but there are so many hearts that still do not open to me.* » This evening let us try to open them: « here is your son. » And Our Mother wants to be with her child, her family and all humanity.

Well, open your hearts this evening in order to fulfill Our Lord's plan, who wanted a community, that we all have a Mother, that we have a bond of love through which Our Lady could speak as a Mother. And the Mother wants to lead us not to Her, but to Jesus because He died for us. It is Her duty to take us, to lead us to Jesus. So let us try be faithful under the Cross, with our Mother, this cross of ours. If we flee from our difficulties and refuse to carry our Cross we will not hear these words: « here I am, here is your Mother. »

By these words I wanted to introduce you to this evening's liturgy, a liturgy I know you will not understand: open your hearts and

Our Lord will talk to you; open your hearts and the word will also be given to you: the word of comfort, of consolation. You will be given grace, because Jesus died for us.

(Fr. Slavko Barbarić - 5th April, 1985)

You must die in order to be resurrected

Yesterday evening, through Ivanka, the visionary to whom Our Lady talks about the problems of the Church and the world, there was a short message: « *You in the parish have got a great and difficult cross, but do not be frightened. My Son will help you carry. it.* » This message is not only for the parish, but for each of us. Messages are usually on Thursdays, but yesterday evening (Good Friday) She gave this message, a word a Mother can say to her children, her sons, her daughters.

She said: « *You have got a great and difficult cross, but do not be frightened. My Son will help you carry it.* »

A message precisely for each of us.

When we are in trouble, Our Lord always wants to help us if we seek this help with an open heart.

Through Jelena She said something that can help us understand this evening's liturgy and also our lives.

Last Saturday Our Lady gave a symbol, an image. She said: « *You all know flowers. A flower must blossom and every part of the flower is very important for the flower. But at a certain moment the flower must fade so that the seed can ripen, and eventually, when it has ripened, other flowers appear.* »

Jelena could not explain this, but it is for the priest to explain: it is very clear. I think that in this, the whole of today's liturgy is contained: you need to die to be able to be resurrected.

Sometimes we say: what a shame, a flower fades. But if it does not, it cannot produce a seed and ripen; the seed from where the other flowers come.

If you do not die you do not multiply life. And if you are not prepared, as Jesus said in the Gospel, to lose your life you cannot look forward to the Resurrection. Also yesterday I reminded the people of what Jesus said from the Cross « Here is your Son, » « here is your Mother. »

And all those who do not want to carry the cross, all those who do not want what Jesus said: « If you want to save your life without taking up your cross you will lose it, » all those who do not want to stay at the foot of the Cross, will never hear this word « here is your Mother. »

The same in this symbol: if we want to save our lives, without God, we will lose them. Our lives will not be multiplied.

This evening the question is this: what is the meaning of dying? It is the same as Our Lord Jesus said: for all of us dying means dying to sin, dying to selfishness, dying to quarrels, dying to the negative side we have got in our hearts.

In this way the life of peace, of love rises once more, a new life full of grace.

So when Our Lord begs us to die, He does not beg, He does not expect us to annihilate ourselves. Our Lord does not want us to be annihilated, but wants us to carry in our hearts the fullness of peace and love.

And during the liturgy which will be in Croatian – some words will also be said for you – let this principle enter your hearts: at some time a flower has to fade to be able to produce a new life.

But look: a flower fades at the right moment. You must not pick it. If a flower is picked from the ground it cannot bring forth the ripe seed. This means for all of us to be always patient with ourselves and with others.

Do not unroot something by means of impatience, hate. You need grace to understand this. During this liturgy may you try to understand with your hearts this concept.

Yesterday in the group, through Jelena, Our Lady said something else that can help: « *Every day you must look for the strength to be able to stand a day like today.* » She was speaking also about Herself and said: « *Rejoice, be of good cheer, because Jesus, my Son, drank His cup.* »

Look, here is also a very important point. If every day we try to die a little bit to sin, to die a bit to the negative side we all have: in what we say, in our actions, in our conduct, we will be strengthened, we will be rooted in Our Lord.

All the difficulties and every time we die will be for us, also a path to resurrection. If we do not travel along this path with Our Lord every day, maybe a difficulty, a trial will show us we are without Our Lord's help. Then these two things: « *You can have joy, because the Lord my Son, drank His cup.* »

An example that must be before our eyes and our hearts: when there is a cup, when there is a cross, we must carry it. Even illness or pain is never given to annihilate us, but to go forward. And I say to you also: cheer up whenever you have drunk a cup, whenever you have had a cross, because by means of the cross Resurrection comes. This morning I spoke with a family who came here a year ago. A child of theirs used to have an allergy and had to receive continuous treatment. But no remedy could be found. They heard about the visionaries, so brought the little girl here: since a year now she has not been having any further discomfort.

I said that when you meet Our Lord you solve also your physical problems. Our Lord has promised also to give signs.

This is the experience of many and I leave it with you, to give you an impulse. Look: if you have opened your hearts Our Lord can do everything with you, inside you. And if He teaches us sometimes that we must die, that we must cry like Jesus yesterday « Father, why did you abandon me? » afterwards resurrection will come.

In the message of 28th March, She said: « *Dear children, pray, pray, pray. In prayer you will have the deepest joy and solve all difficult situations, the ones that look impossible to you.* »

This is very important too. Praying means meeting Our Lord and when we meet one who is almighty, who loves us, who lets Himself be called Father by us there is no situation that cannot be solved. Not by us, but by Our Lord in us.

This is the very thing Our Lady wants of all of us: She wants us to be ready to die to sin and to be resurrected to peace, to reconciliation.

In a message (14th March) She said: « *Many are those coming to you: give them light, dear children.* » There is nobody all over the world who does not want peace but there are not many who give it: who give light, who offer themselves as love.

During these days we must learn this and above all, those of us present how to give light. And when you go back home, to your families, to work, to school, to your studies, rather than wanting to be loved or wanting others to give you peace: give peace, love others and you will see that life is more beautiful, because Jesus has risen. Now pray. Let this flower live in your hearts, then die and bring forth fruit again.

(Fr. Slavko Barbarić - 6th April, 1985)

« I invite you to the light you must bring to all those who are in darkness »

Lent messages

While wishing you all a Happy Easter, I want to introduce you to the Lent messages in this period.

On Thursday before Lent February 14, She said: « *Today is the day I usually give you messages. But all the Parish does not accept and live them. I am sad and would like you, dear children, to listen to my messages and to live them. Every family must pray together and read the Bible. Thank you for your response to my call.* »

I can add this to the message. We do not know many messages in which Our Lady says « you must, » but in this message She said it. Our Lady always introduces herself as the Mother who knocks and who you have to open the door to. And if Our Lady says « you must, » you really must take this word seriously.

And this was, I think, the preparation for Lent.

Our Lady teaches us. She wanted to prepare us for Lent after saying « *you must pray and read the Bible.* »

On the first Thursday (21st February) She said: « *Dear children, day after day I invite you to renew your prayer in the parish. But you do not accept. Today I am inviting you for the last time: Lent has begun and you, as a parish, can arouse yourselves to my call for my sake. If you do not do so I do not wish to give any more messages. Our Lord lets me do this. Thank you for your response to my call.* »

Another little explanation. Our Lady said « *I invite you for the last time.* » Then She does not say « you must » any longer. She invites us again: « *for my sake you should answer my call. If you do not want to, I will not speak.* » She does not want to force us. I say this: if love does not arouse us, what can? Fear? If we wait for fear it can even be too late. I think it is better to answer the invitation of love than the one of fear. And if we answer only for fear we act still as children who understand only when you shake your finger.

On 28th February She gave the following message: *« Dear children, today I am inviting you to live, all the week long, these words "I love God". Dear children, through love you can succeed in everything, even in what seems impossible to you. Our Lord wants a total abandonment of the Parish to Him... I want it too. Thank you for your response to my call. »*

So when She said *« if you do not want it I will speak no more, »* we did not know whether She would still give messages. But then Our Lady gave this wonderful message by which She invited us to live the words *« I love God »*: this is very important. By these words *« I love God »* we can always examine, every day, our whole life long. And we must always look at all words, all actions under these words *« I love God. »*

She said another thing: *« by love you can win everything, even impossible things. »* So, if we have some difficulties, this is a sign that our love is still shallow. This is something we must always think of. Can I live all my life under these words: I love God?

On 7th March She gave this message: *« Dear children, I invite you to the renewal of prayer in your families. Dear children, invite the youngest to prayer and to the celebration of Mass. Thank you for your response to my call. »*

So here She invites the relatives to pray with the little ones.

This is most important. There is a saying: The very things the grown-ups do not do, the young can learn less easily or they cannot learn them at all. And if you do not pray, how can the young?

But if you begin, you relatives, you grown-ups, to pray, children will pray, and the young too.

And if you meet Our Lord in prayer and you are joyful the young will follow you. So, instead of getting angry with the young, pray in front of them.

Another message on 14th March: « *Dear children, in life you will have the experience of light and of darkness. Our Lord gives everybody the gift of recognising, of discerning good from evil. I invite you to the light which you must bring to all those who live in darkness. Every day people who are in darkness come to your homes. Give them, dear children, light. Thank you for your response to my call.* »

Starting from this message I want to say this; Our Lady invites us to give light to all those who are in darkness. I am sure every man on earth wants peace, wants love, wants light.

But we all know that there is still not much love in the world, much peace, much reconciliation.

And we all wonder why? The answer is this: there are not yet many who can give this. From whom can we expect peace and love, but from the ones who know Jesus, who know Our Lady? So, when you go back to your families and to your homes, do not try to be loved, but to love.

Do not seek peace from the others, but give it. And you will see: they all want peace and will be willing to accept it. And this is our duty. Give light, because we accept it from Our Lord.

On 21st March She gave this message: « *Dear children, today I am inviting you: pray, pray, pray. In prayer you will have the deepest joy and the solution to every situation that seems impossible to you. Thank you for having become active in prayer. Each of you is dear to my heart. I thank all those who have encouraged prayer in their families.* »

She says: « *In prayer you will have the deepest joy* » So, where is your joy?, Again we must wonder: what is our prayer? Prayer means meeting Our Lord personally. If we do not have joy, maybe we cannot pray well, maybe our prayer is only a mechanical prayer. And I know that nobody is against the deepest joy. So why not take time for the deepest prayer and learn it?

Because this is the path to the deepest joy.

A message not dating Thursday, but Sunday (24th March), The

83

Eve of the Annunciation was: « *Today I want to invite you to Confession. Even if you have been to confession recently I want you to live my feast-day in your hearts. But you cannot live it if you are not completely abandoned to Our Lord. For this reason I invite you to be reconciled to the Lord.* »

Just a word: what does « reconciliation » mean?

« Reconciliation » means accepting Our Lord's will which we refused in sin. We refused in sin Our Lord's plan for us. And Our Lady invites us to accept this plan coming from Our Lord, as She did on the day of the Annunciation. Our Lady said « yes. » It can be said that Her « fiat » was Her reconciliation. She was ready to accept.

On Maundy Thursday: « *Dear children, I thank you because you have begun thinking more of Our Lord's glory in your hearts. Today is the day when I did not want to give any more messages because some of you do not accept me. But the Parish has made a move and for this reason I want to continue giving you also in the future, my messages in a way that has never happened in the history of the world.* »

What is the meaning of thinking of Our Lord's glory? Seeking peace, love, reconciliation. That is what this means. This is what Our Lord wants. Our Lady said She did not want to give any more messages.

I think She said that, you know, because of the difficulties we are having. But She said: « *as you accept them, I am going on giving them.* »

This is a sign for us that Our Lady will win with God's children. And you are God's children.

On Good Friday She gave a message through Ivanka: « *You in the Parish are having a great and difficult cross: but do not be afraid of carrying it. Here is My Son who will help you.* »

Not only to the Parish, but to you all She said: « *My Son is with you and will help you carry the Cross.* »

These were the Lent messages.

(Fr. Slavko Barbarić - 7th April, 1985)

Our Lady taught us to take three steps forward in group prayer

I would like to say a few words about my experience in these last few days when really living Good Friday and Easter.

Last year, on Holy Saturday, I received a particular present, very small, but interesting. An orthodox convert came to me bringing a present and saying: « I want to give you a present and you know what it is. If I bring you money you will say: I do not need it. I have brought you the key to my house, so that you can enter my house whenever you like. I do not know whether you are going to come to my home, but I am happy to give you the key of my house and to know that you may enter it whenever you like. »

You see: the same happened today, all of us received this present. We received the key of our heavenly home. And it is important to understand that with this key which we have received, we can open every door. We can open every problem and solve it. What we have to say today, is that we must begin living this reality.

We have actually received the key of the heavenly door, which means of all the doors of human problems. The Resurrection solves every problem.

Yesterday I read a postcard from a sick nun, who is going to die in a few days. She writes « you cannot understand my joy because the day is approaching when I will meet my Heavenly Father. »

So you see: if we have accepted this key of the heavenly door and live it, even the greatest difficulties in our lives are of no account. We are happy because of the joy and life to come.

And I think that we can understand Our Lady and Her message of peace only if we accept, to-day, this key, because in the light of the Resurrection all problems are solved, if we adopt the same attitude as Mary Magdalen and say: God is everything for me. If God becomes everything for me, then I use this key of the Resurrection. I will tell you how you can use it: you must be crucified. I would be very sad if today Our Heavenly Father should come back to us full of sadness. He offered everything, He gave us even His Son and we cannot accept this immense gift if we do not extinguish our sins: even a little sin, even a touch of sin prevents us from living this reality.

I want to tell you this, so that you may go on during these days. I say go on, because this day, the Resurrection, is only the first day of the Resurrection; then you will have to live a second, third... and fortieth one, because Lent lasts forty days, but Easter time lasts forty days too. So we have to walk forty days in the light of the Resurrection and if you begin living this key of faith, then after forty days you will be really changed.

By the way, I must tell particularly the pilgrims and the leaders coming here several times, to go on going deeper into the meaning of the messages of prayer.

When we say going deeper into the meaning of the messages about prayer I can see two very important aspects: first, my prayer must become more and more recollected. I have to go inside myself, into the messages, listen to them, understand them: my prayer must become more and more recollected. I must hear God's voice inside my conscience.

On the other hand, my prayer must become every day more and more active towards my neighbour, towards achieving what I have understood in prayer, achieving it in relation to others.

The last time I said that Our Lady insisted on frequent confession, She said, however, that if you go to confession without achieving it in relation to others, your confession is not complete. In this sense – if I have offended somebody and I do not achieve what I have confessed, confession has not brought forth its fruit.

Now, for prayer groups, this opening to humility is very important, when the group acknowledges its own weaknesses, because when the group confesses, not sacramental confession, but the confession of their own lives, everybody becomes one in humility and in their opening towards God. So God can then proceed further.

Last time Our Lady taught us to take three steps forward in group prayer.

The first step is UNBURDENING EVERY SIN AND EVERY RESENTMENT OF ONE'S SINS, they must truly be put aside. Without this step we will not enter into prayer. We only reach the beginning and the pang of conscience is repeated, the analysis of sins is repeated.

We must leave our sins aside, confess them and, at the same time, to LEAVE OUR CARES TO GOD.

When we have taken this step we enter freedom, we are in touch with God.

Now, the Holy Ghost speaks to us because we are free and, in this second step, we pray for God's plans, because a clean and free heart can understand what God plans inside us. If we have not taken this step forward, then we cannot progress in prayer, for, as the Virgin said to Jelena: « *A lot of Christians in daily prayer only reach the beginning of prayer but go no further.* »

The third stage of prayer is to ASK FOR BLESSING. But when we speak of blessing we do not mean something magic. Our Lady speaks of something real. When in the divine plan of prayer I saw what God wants of me, then I start achieving this. God gives me the strength and I understand His blessing as the strength to achieve what God wants of me. At the same time I must take, accept and cherish this blessing like a precious pearl.

Several times Our Lady said to us: « *You receive the blessing, then you forget it.* »

Now you can see that all these three points are to be developed every day, to be improved every day, so when we speak about improvement in prayer, we mean actually improving these three elements. If you try to improve these three elements your prayer will become continuous. If you want to cherish the divine blessing inside yourselves you must pray constantly, that is bring prayer into your everyday life and if you want to be able to enter into prayer, you must achieve what prayer requires of you; if you do that, you will be happy.

Perhaps these words are too many. We are used to uttering too many words also, we priests. I am only going to say: go on in prayer, go on into the depth of prayer. As you go into the depth of prayer, so the divine light will increase.

Several people told me during these days: I want faith. But anyone can have faith; but it depends on you. Faith means taking a step forward. I cannot see the town from the other side of the mountain: I have to climb. If I want to have a greater light, in my faith, I have to take the steps I understand.

There is no need to ask for advice, as people do in the confessional; this advice is already in the Gospel and we all can understand it. You need to take those steps that are in the Gospel: so the light will become brighter.

I wish that this day of Resurrection may be only the beginning of a beautiful life for you all. Have a good journey. And best wishes.

(Fr. Tomislav Vlašić - 7th April, 1985)

Many stop at Easter and do not live the Resurrection

This day is very beautiful for me. You too can realize that apparitions are necessary. The Church needs apparitions. One stage in Jesus' life ended a short time ago. Now we cannot drive people forward without apparitions. The Resurrected Christ appeared. This is one of the stages in Christian life without which you cannot go forward.

The Apostles could not go on without Jesus' apparitions. It is a stage in the life of the Church that must take its course. After the apparitions comes the Holy Spirit.

These are stages we must follow in our spiritual life.

I think you have understood this.

Because the Apostles could understand certain truths only after Jesus had risen and appeared to them, this apparition gave them a new sensitivity and they could see what their physical eyes had not been able to perceive previously. At last the Holy Spirit came to make them understand the truth, the whole truth.

We must follow this same path just as the Apostles did. Therefore, we must not wonder at the apparitions in the Church. They are required because the Church must always walk this same path as the Apostles did. Which is the same path the primitive Church walked.

We call this day Emmaus' day and people usually go to visit other people.

People have changed the day after Easter into a day devoted to visits while the Christian truth is quite different. When Jesus rose He became our fellow traveller and we must carry on living with Him.

Yesterday is a day which reminds us of the Resurrection. It is the first day of the Resurrection. To-day we must walk with Jesus. We prepare ourselves for Easter during Lent, but very few remember that after Easter we must walk forty days to live the Resurrection, to reach the third stage.

In my opinion we must live these forty days with the same intensity as during Lent, but with joy. Then, if we go forward with Jesus, with joy, we will enter the third stage, the one of the Holy Spirit.

Most Christians stop at Easter and do not live the Resurrection. When a seed germinates and sprouts it produces grass; from the grain comes the grass with the strength to bear new fruit.

Most Christians see the light and then fade away. These forty days should be used to open the door to life and be filled with the strength coming from the Risen Christ. In this way the strength of the Risen Christ will be manifested and in the third stage we will be ready to proclaim the Risen Christ, as we heard in to-day's liturgy. What has happened? Some people wanted to dismiss the Resurrection. They were paid to do so, the soldiers were bribed. Jesus says to the women « go and announce it. » Look, if we have understood the Resurrection we must go and announce it. And what if we are not yet ready? The Apostles were also not ready. They withdrew to pray for nine days during those forty days and to live a true godlike life so that they might be able to announce the Good News.

Do this and you will be overflowing with the grace of the Risen Christ. During these last days I have come to understand certain things necessary in order to help live Jesus' Resurrection. The first thing is to have the sin which is in us totally destroyed. As long as there is even a shade of sin we cannot live the Resurrection.

As long as there is sin inside us and we have not lived the Resurrection within and have not experienced the divine love, we are not in a position to accept it. Therefore, the sin will be destroyed in proportion to how we were able to live the Good Friday and to this extent will we be able to live Jesus Christ's Resurrection.

I will give you a picture: if you look at a blood-soaked person dead on the road, it is a terrible sight. So you see, when someone kills another and experiences this feeling, it is something horrible. But if they do not feel anything, even if the one who is going to be killed tells him that he loves him with all his heart, he does not understand and that is why he kills.

Now you can realise how the hardness of our hearts is in the same proportion to the sin which kills Him.

To the same extent that my heart lives the sin, my heart kills Jesus; it cannot feel His Resurrection, it cannot mourn Good Friday, nor rejoice at the moment of the Resurrection.

This is, therefore, the picture following the death of Jesus. « Rocks opened up, split and the heart of man still remained hard. »

So you see: we must now continue along this path if we want to live Jesus' Resurrection during these forty days.

At the same time we must go on living our Good Friday.

The Cross destroys sin; if we accept it with love we approach Jesus' Resurrection.

This negative side of the destruction of the sin which is in ourselves is in the same proportion to our acceptance of Jesus rising from the dead. At the same time we must be aware that the measure by which we can live and experience the Resurrection is the same measure by which we proclaim Jesus Christ.

To-day I spoke to people and said to those who came: « You are happy. » I felt this in my heart. Now, after the Resurrection we are happy because Jesus is walking in this world, no longer in a human body, but in His resurrected body and he can enter even through a closed door, he can reach us everywhere.

As a matter of fact, consider the Gospel after the Resurrection. He goes to Galilee, he meets the Apostles on the sea, He meets them everywhere on the roads, and, if you want to understand the days after the Resurrection, these are the days when Jesus is everywhere. He is the friend who accompanies you everywhere and when you are in difficulties, you will know that he can enter your hearts through difficulties, even through the difficulty of death. And this is the peace, the root of peace. Now glorified Jesus offers us this grace; to enter inside ourselves even if there are difficult obstacles.

He who lives in faith does not undergo a crisis; he may have trials. It is very important to understand this attitude. People who stand firm in their faith only on the basis of exterior concepts, of exterior studies, always lag; they get lost when detail is lacking. But the foundation of faith cannot be justified by exterior reasoning. The basis of faith is a total abandonment to God carrying us through difficulties and through the Cross (which is also foolish for unbelievers, according to S. Paul), carrying us also beyond the concept that the Blessed Virgin did conceive. And this cannot be justified by human reasoning. And when people have found this abandonment they find the interior light that enlightens and they never lag behind. When trials, not crises, come, they feel very sure that God's hand will lead them forward whatever the situation.

Now I should like you to be the messanger of this inward strength, of this inward certainty, so that those who believe in the apparitions may be staunch to faith and not to human reasoning.

Otherwise, if you base yourselves on human reasoning you will be like St. Peter when he walked on the water and began to sink... while Jesus taught to have faith, because with human reasoning we cannot walk on water, but with the strength of faith we can walk even on air, not only on water.

This is very important, because the messages you have heard from Medjugorje are the messages you know by heart, by now.

If I say to you: « pray, » you have already learnt it by heart, but that is too little.

Therefore, I often tell the pilgrims: those who want to follow Our Lady must go beyond the messages. The messages are the call, they are the arrows, they are the words that carry us forward. They bind us to live the Gospel just like the Blessed Virgin lived it. I want, now, to finish with this message of peace which comes from lived faith.

There are some people who say to me: « I would like to have faith and peace in God, » and I always say to them: « accept it. » « But how can I accept it? I always want it more and more... »

I replied: « If you want to have more faith, go forward. » The town beyond the mountain cannot be seen from the opposite side. We must walk on, and then the horizon widens.

The faith Jesus speaks of is not a fixed idea, but rather a pilgrimage together with God. A person grows by living the messages, by taking the Gospel as a basis, following it and by opening up more and more to faith. Faith then increases inside the person.

This also happens when you speak of peace and love.

To-day I spoke to a person who asked me how he could love his enemies.

I said to him: « It is very easy. First of all you must love yourself in Jesus Christ. You must discover Jesus Christ, in the Gospel, who loves you. You must experience divine love and when you have truly experienced this you are saved, you are filled, you become like an overflowing cup. »

Then no effort is required, everything goes by itself, even love towards your enemies.

It does not matter to the sun if there are clouds. The sun shines all the same and our task is to live the strength of love, of light, of the peace which is in Jesus Christ.

Then we can understand what Jesus wanted: to bring the Gospel to others. We must understand that we must not bring people just words, messages, but life. Now if there is life inside me I can carry it. If there is the redemption inside me, if all my wounds have healed, it is not difficult for me to love my enemies. Indeed, I need to love and I have the strength to love them, to embrace them.

So set forth on the path of the Resurrection. It is very easy. I say so because a lot of people ask: how can I get there? It is the same as when a child says: I would like to become a friar but I could never bring myself to go into the pulpit and preach. The child must walk, must set out and take the first steps.

Results are lacking only because people do not set out, do not start day by day taking the first small steps that the Church has shown them; the steps of daily prayer and of Holy Communion. The small simple steps in order to bring us to live the Sacraments. I will try to follow you with my daily prayer, but if you open your hearts to Jesus you will not be lacking in graces.

Question: Actually, what does it mean to open our hearts? Not to offer resistance, not to set limits to what is requested of us?

Answer: Yes, in broad terms it is that. But for every question which is asked, for every subject, there must be a very wide answer. No one can receive the answer on a theoretical level.

To open ourselves means to set out, to be alert and to accept every divine word. If you want to have an answer to this opening... You will always get it through silence and prayer. Namely, the capacity to grasp in silence what God says to us in our hearts. Without this there is something lacking about this « opening. »

On one hand, there is the opening towards silence, towards a very deep peace in which we can hear the Holy Spirit, the Gospel and on the other hand our opening goes forward towards our neighbour. If I feel a certain tension towards someone, I cannot be completely open. If I do not love one of you I cannot be open. If I am aggressive because I have seen something on television, I am already closed. One has to be open towards God and open to one's neighbour and then our opening of love is complete, our opening towards God is complete.

If you want to experience this, read the passages of St. Matthew, Ch. 5-6,7, throughout your lifetime, for you will find this sufficient for your whole life.

(Fr. Tomislav Vlašić - 8th April, 1985)

The first thing to understand is the Will of God, even in suffering

Welcome to everyone. The apparitions still come every evening. Every evening, Ivanka, Vicka, Jacov, Marija and Ivan still see Our Lady.

They have been seeing her for 46 months; by the 24th April it will be 46 months.

It is already a long story. None of us ever dared to wish for anything like this. Apparitions like this are unknown in the history of the Church. And everybody keeps wondering how on earth is it possible? And we too wonder how it is possible.

But what can we do with these five (originally six) who have said from the first evening until today « we see Our Lady »?

And they are personally sorely tried, and not only they, but also the Parish and the Franciscan community have had a lot of trouble and trials, but the contact with Our Lady goes on in spite of all our problems. Even today, we are in trouble, but we feel secure because we have learnt a lot from our past history, we have learnt that Our Lady will find new solutions, and that from these we shall emerge purified. But we can see here that every cross, every difficult situation does not come to destroy us but to make us rise again. And this is the first message for all of you, for all of us.

All the crosses you have to bear, all the troubles you have, do not come to destroy, they are not in your lives to destroy but to help you rise again. For example, the message that Our Lady gave through Ivanka on Good Friday is this: « *All of you in the Parish have a heavy and difficult cross to bear, but do not be afraid to bear it. My Son is here and He will help you.* »

What is said for the Parish is said for all of you, you are the Parish. And so I repeat: of course there are many who come here for cures – physical or psychical cures, but I tell you that the first thing to look for is the Will of God, that His Will be done even in trouble, sickness, or in suffering.

So, in any situation, we must look for and try to do the Will of God. And this is the meaning of the message of the 24th March, the eve of the Annunciation.

Our Lady said: « *Today I invite you to make your confession, even if you have already done so recently. I want you to live my feast day in your hearts, but you cannot live it without giving yourselves completely to God. I invite you to reconcile yourselves with God.* »

To be reconciled in this situation, said on the eve of the feast of the Annunciation, is deeply significant.

To be reconciled with God does not only mean forgiving someone; the deep meaning is to accept God's plan for us with all our lives. We lost this reconciliation with God when we began to sin in the earthly paradise; when man said: I do not want to follow you – I will go my own way.

Our Lady invites us to reconciliation on the day she herself consciously said « Yes » to Our Lord. She had her own programme, her plan for her life, she was engaged to be married. God came to her and said to her « You shall be the Mother of Jesus. »

She did not understand but she said « Yes. »

This is reconciliation and this is also the meaning of peace, of conversion – accepting the Will of God.

That is why we say when you come here and when you want to live the message Our Lady has given, the only thing you must do now and always is to live the Will of God. The Will of God is hard for us of course, but in another message, she said: « *Accept me, dear children, and then you will be happy.* » Everything Our Lady asks for is for our good.

Then in a message given to Jelena, she said: « *Dear children, I am saved but I want you to be saved too.* »

A very important message is that of the 28th March when she said « *Pray, pray, pray. You will find your greatest joy in prayer.* »

No one amongst us is against this joy, the greatest.

And so no one refuses joy, we search for it all our lives. But why do we so often not find it?

Perhaps the reason is that we do not yet know how to pray.

And from this message we can see what is meant by prayer. Prayer is a way of meeting Our Lord, and meeting Him is very important. On a human level, if you want to meet someone, you must have time for him, sit down, have a coffee or eat and talk, see what he wants, how he is, listen to his problems and tell him yours too; this is a meeting, at least on a human level.

To be able to pray, to feel a deeper joy, one must take time for prayer. Prayer does not mean just saying a Hail Mary or an Our Father, it means meditating in your hearts.

The prayers asked for in these apparitions are: The Creed and seven Our Father's, the whole Rosary, monthly confession, the Mass and fasting. At the beginning Our Lady asked for one day of fasting and as from August, 1984, two days.

How you fast and if you fast, I do not know. It does not interest me. What I want to tell you though is what Our Lady wishes. When she wishes for something, it is for our good. Prayer is the way to feel a deeper joy and peace. Fasting, too, is a way. We do not fast for fasting's sake and we know that fasting is first of all a service for the faith.

You must be very careful. Our Lady has announced atheism and here we can say that she is fighting against atheism, our practical atheism. We are all a bit atheist and when Our Lady asks for fasting, she is asking us to live two days a week like poor people before the Lord.

Fasting means leaving everything and opening our hearts to God. Our Lady also fasted two days a week because it was the custom to do so in the early Church, on Wednesdays and Fridays. And Our Lady lived like the early Church.

So we must open our hearts and wait only for God.

The Holy Fathers say fasting is the prayer of our body. This connection between fasting and faith means that if one is poor, one cannot ever say « I do not need you. » The poor in spirit will never say to Our Lord « I do not need you. » They are open to Him.

Atheism enters into us when our love is full of our plans and projects, and our thoughts are then closed to God, then we become atheists.

There is another characteristic of fasting – it sets in motion a process of purification. In this materialistic world, we become blind because of the things we have and always want more of.

The heart of man knows no bounds to this desire to have, unless he can find them in the process of purification.

To be purified of these possessive desires, wanting only to have. Fasting helps and if we begin and if we go on, we will realise two things: that we have enough and that there is no need for much fear and anguish about how to live, and we shall see that thousands all over the world are, at this moment, dying of hunger or are without the bare necessities for life.

Our Lady, as Mother of all, invites us to share, to give; but fasting is not giving something to others. A poor man has to fast, too, so as not to feel the bitterness of his poverty, to be free even in poverty.

One does not ask a poor man for money for others.

A rich man must fast, live on bread so as to be able to see the others, to be able to see that he, too, needs to feel near Our Lord, in spite of his riches. Therefore, we can say that prayer and fasting are as fundamental to our lives as Christians, as breathing and eating are to our physical lives. When we breathe and eat, our lives develop according to our situation.

Our Lady begins like this and gives us the means of living as Christians who feel and listen and love God above everything else and love their neighbours as themselves.

But we cannot discuss fasting for long; Let me give you some advice! Begin to fast and you will see.

Just recently I had an interview with a professor of spirituality for a newspaper, a convert. We also talked about fasting and he said: « I know that fasting helps me, I know that when I fast, I can pray much better and have more time for myself, for God and for the others. I am happy to have discovered this. »

So many people tell me they cannot fast. A pilgrim said: « I am ashamed to meet Fr. Tomislav because once in confession he asked me if I fasted and I said I could not. »

And he answered: « Yes, I can believe that you cannot start, but I do not believe you cannot try! » After some months, she said « I am ashamed to meet Fr. Tomislav, because I realise that I can fast even three days a week and still feel well. »

Then she said something else: « I am happier and my family has become quite different. Now I see that there is no reason to be worried if I live on bread for a day. I save many things. If I live like this for one day, I am more open for many other things. »

And so I say « Try! » if you cannot do it, it is not a sin to try! Our Lady asks for an ideal, one can say, and we must gradually stretch towards this ideal.

But again I say: do not fast just for the sake of fasting.

Do you know the story of the Pharisee to whom Jesus said: you already have your recompense when the Pharisee said to Him: I fast twice and pray and give alms. So I am better than this man in the corner.

So he judged: I can, the other cannot.

No, we do not pray so as to pass judgement on those who do not, we do not fast in order to pass judgement on those who do not. I pray, I fast because in this way I can meet Our Lord, I can feel His presence more and I am more open to others, too.

One thing I want to conclude with is this: in one of her inner conversations with Our Lady, Jelena asked Her: « Why are you so beautiful? » The answer was: « *Because I love. If you wish to become beautiful, you must love.* » Wonderful advice.

There is no one in the world who does not wish to be beautiful, even when they have faces that only a mother can love. All of us would like to be beautiful and to become so, we must begin to love, to open our hearts to love. One can live with someone who loves, who is ready to be reconciled even if they do not really have external beauty. As for inner beauty, we all have the chance of it; this chance is always with us and in us.

A beautiful mother wishes to have beautiful children: this is why Our Lady came and has stayed so long with us.

We all know that it is not easy to love, but love is not a word, it is a life. It means forgiving, seeing others, visiting the sick; all this means love. If we say it is difficult, it does not mean that it is worthless; the difficult things are so often the worthwhile things, the valuable things. I also wish, in the name of the Parish, of the visionaries, in the name of Our Lady whom we cannot see but whom we feel, that you may have the experience when she said: « *Pray, pray, pray. It is in prayer that you will feel the deepest joy.* »

Not just beginning today but going on when you go back to your families. Last year, after Easter, Our Lady said: « *There are so many sick who have not received graces because they stopped praying when they got back to their homes.* »

We must go on with prayer and fasting and open our hearts and look for the Will of God. When we do this we are sure Our Lord will always be with us.

(Fr. Slavko Barbarić - 10th April, 1985)

The apparitions are a stage in the spiritual life of the Church

First of all I would like all of you to give the other pilgrims the message that Medjugorje is going through trials, but not crises. These trials are something which must come, and if there is deep conversion, then the trials are greater.

If at Medjugorje, we had declared that Our Lady had appeared right from the beginning, this would be no good. It would have been just a statement, but conversion is a path, a therapy. When our bodies need healing, the diseased part must be opened up so that we can see what is the matter inside and heal it. If God wishes to bring the Church and the world to conversion, all those who wish to follow this road will have to go through difficulties.

Recently I read some mystical books and I liked the message Jesus gave to a Swiss mystic who was a convert; He said « Gentle Providence takes care to provide you with bread every day. But when you ask for virtue, then my gentle Providence gives you crosses to bear so that you may acquire virtue. »

He puts bread and the cross in that order; without the cross, we cannot grow. As if it were nourishment for spiritual life.

I have experienced it: if you wish to go forward, you must expect crosses. But the crosses do not bring you bitterness, they bring sweetness and peace. And here we realise that human life develops along two planes: on the materialistic plane we live a material and consumer life; life draws in and ends in death. On the spiritual plane, life opens out more and more all the time; the dynamic spring of life, happiness, love and inner peace. So even if people finish on the cross, life becomes fuller.

The Resurrection of Jesus Christ is not an isolated fact; it is like a river, when life was extinguished in the Garden of Olives and on the Cross, it was not lost: it is like a river which goes underground to come out again. Along the Way of the Cross, Jesus never lost anything of His spirit; He was waiting all the time; He forgave and gave consolation. He gave consolation while carrying the Cross, He forgave while He was crucified; life was full even on the Cross.

For those who wish to pursue a spiritual life right to the end, there will be crosses. If we accept them with God, they do not diminish our lives, they give strength and life becomes stronger within us. This is the line we must follow now.

I have told many pilgrims that we Christians are making a mistake. We follow Jesus during Lent for forty days, we fast a little, we give up a few things and say a few more prayers, but when Easter comes, it often ends within the day. Easter time goes on for forty days.

It is a stage in spiritual life; to go with Jesus, who has risen, for forty days, so that each one of us may be woken and be resurrected. Jesus is risen. This was not enough. Jesus went to search for the Apostles and the women to give them new life. He stayed with them for forty days for the Spirit to be reborn within them. And in the third stage, the Holy Spirit will come to give us light.

This tells me that this Easter is a wonderful time for understanding the apparitions of Our Lady, too.

After the death of Jesus Christ, it was important for salvation that He should show Himself to the Apostles. The apparitions are a stage in the spiritual life of the Church and of each one of us. Apparitions in the history of salvation, in the history of the Church go on bringing us towards a state of mind in which we shall be spiritually resurrected and become capable of accepting the Holy Spirit.

This period of time is very beautiful if you accept it like this, as the risen Jesus wanted.

The first words He said to the Apostles were: « Peace be unto you. » They are the same words said at Medjugorje. But when one says: « Peace be with you, » it may sound empty. It is not just any word which appears in the newspapers, it is a profound reality.

Jesus walked with the Apostles on earth, in His physical body, He did everything to convince them. After the Resurrection, He came closer. It is His body which enters even through closed doors, which enters into every man, into every problem, if people are ready to call Him. So there is no longer even that physical difficulty to prevent us from meeting Jesus. He found the Apostles closed, even spiritually closed, perhaps because they were disappointed, they didn't know what to do. They were even in a closed room. But this is only to understand that we too, with all our problems, also have Jesus who brings us peace: « Do not worry, I can resolve all your problems. Open your hearts. I have come to save you. »

When we understand this, we reach a fundamental attitude, a spiritual one. If you want to understand better, you will see that after the Apostles, St. Paul for instance, while he was in prison, shut in, guarded, was full of joy, he praised the Lord and prayed. And the doors opened, his chains fell away – he was free.

Jesus is the Master of life!

Now you will see how important it is to live this Easter time, live it more intensely than Lent, to be resurrected, to live this spiritual reality. We can reflect on a message from Our Lady, when she is speaking about prayer and says: « *Prayer must be a rejoicing in God, thriving in God. To be full of peace, to be full of joy.* »

Every prayer, then, should be a resurrection if, during this time of resurrection, we walk with Jesus who walked with us.

We shall reach a much stronger inner attitude, spiritually, and we shall be capable of accepting the Holy Spirit. And then everything will become clear. Many people ask me this question: « How can we reach a stronger faith? How can we manage to pray more deeply? »

Many worry about how to reach their goal, but forget to make the steps. Faith is not knowledge of a truth. From below the mountain, you cannot see a city on the other side; you have to start walking and climb up the mountain to see the city.

It is the same thing with faith, with prayer and with spiritual life; you must put one foot in front of the other, you must start walking. If you want to make a step forward, then God will open the way;

if you take two steps God will open out your horizon more and more. To ask for faith means to walk in faith. To ask for the gift of prayer means to walk with prayer, to practise prayer. To ask for greater recollection means to go towards it and to put aside everything that prevents it.

In this way, faith becomes very easy and one need not worry about when the end will come; I must follow the steps, I must be with faith now, walking in the way of the Lord.

I want to remind you of something which will be very useful to you in living this Easter time. We shall be able to live the Easter time insofar as we shall have wiped out our sin, insofar as Good Friday has happened within ourselves, if we have crucified our ego.

Recently I was reading an interview with a young American pedagogue who had dedicated himself to handicapped children. Amongst other things, he said: « My greatest sorrow is when I go back home weeping because I have left children crying. The children cry because they do not understand my love. They understand it as pity, not as pure love, because they have been disillusioned in their parents. This disillusionment, the sin of their parents is inside them and they are incapable of accepting the love of others, as they have not accepted love. »

I thought about it and I said to the people: perhaps God the Father will come back to us weeping at this Easter time, when He gave us all, absolutely all; He even offered His Son, He gave Him to be crucified, because we are incapable of accepting, we have not lived Good Friday, we have not crucified ourselves; we have not destroyed sin.

If we wish to walk with Jesus during this Easter time, we must live Good Friday every day within ourselves, really destroy sin; not even the shadow of sin must be left in us.

Then it will be easy to meet the risen Jesus and to understand all that God does today in the world; it will also be easy to understand the apparitions of Our Lady and, living this time, we shall be able to understand the spiritual themes.

Examined from the outside, even scientifically, the apparitions at Medjugorje, like every other apparition, will not yield results.

Those people who are limited to solely scientific fields, will always limp along because rational themes, rational arguments can never justify spiritual themes, those concerning faith.

We have not enough human reasoning to understand the conception of the Virgin; how can a virgin conceive?

How can we understand that Jesus said to Peter: « Walk on the water? »

It is not something we can accept, we have no explanation.

How can we understand that the Son of God could be put on the Cross?

Human arguments are not enough in spiritual life to understand the apparitions. There must be an inner progress. The messages given by Our Lady are the path to understanding the apparitions and the path to salvation. Only those who try this path can understand, because they will feel the fruits Our Lady offers through divine grace immediately or very soon.

With all this I wanted to tell you that there is no need to ask for extraordinary items of news at Medjugorje. I have followed and still follow what Our Lady said; every thing can be reduced to « Get up, open your hearts, open your eyes; look, pray, do not go to sleep. »

She does what a mother does to look after her child, her children. There are no extraordinary principles, she does everything with simplicity and humility; she draws close to humanity and says « Go forward! »

What we must understand and emphasise, and what the visionaries emphasise, is that the events announced by Our Lady are coming nearer.

I cannot speak about this, but we can all understand it if we really try seriously to see humanity as it is, and what is written in the Gospels. We will then be able to understand what Our Lady means, not anxiously but joyfully, because our every step is close to the Father and at the same time close to happiness.

I must say that all the difficulties along the way as, for instance, certain obstacles can only be overcome by prayer, by love.

External reasoning does little or nothing. I have experienced this.

When we abandon ourselves to God and pray, God easily moves both things and people. Human reasoning cannot enlighten human hearts. Therefore, I ask all the pilgrims to pray for Our Lady's work, so that, through Her, the divine plan may be fully accomplished.

I want to add that those who wish to heed the apparitions must understand that they must go beyond the messages. The messages are empty words unless we go beyond them. « Prayer » is a word which we have known for a long time, but we must go further; if we start practising it we shall understand it more. Now I see, I understand certain things I did not understand at the beginning. If we go forward this inner light grows in us.

The apparitions are an appeal to the world to reflect, to enter into the Gospel and, when the Gospel is understood, then also the apparitions can be understood. Half way through Lent, Our Lady taught us to pray saying the Our Father in a prayer group. For hours and hours, we prayed, saying only the Our Father. As in the messages, and through little Jelena too Our Lady has pointed out that in a prayer group it is important to make three steps; the first is to be emptied of every sin; it is not enough to go to the confessional because, according to her teaching, one must live a prolonged confession. I must behave as a friend with you.

If I am afraid before someone, I must tell of my weakness. If I feel oppressed by something which closes me to you, I must put it away from me, I must free myself from all sin and from the shadow of sin.

Before praying, the group or the person must make this first step and throw off every sin which is a disturbing element.

The second thing is to be free from all worries. Give all your worries and problems to Jesus. After this step, one finds inner freedom and enters into prayer.

As Our Lady said: *« Many Christians never enter into prayer. They manage to begin and then stay at the beginning. »*

There are many people who pray, who are full of anxiety, remorse, and analysis of sins etc. ...

But all this must be unloaded at the beginning and when we enter into prayer, we enter into a divine plan which is in our hearts and then it is the Holy Spirit who prays within us, as St. Paul says to the Romans: « Now that we are free from sin, free from worry, now we can enter into prayer. »

All this is a preparation for prayer.

It is not easy, but we must go forward, we must understand it in groups and in private. And all this is done through prayer. For example, a nun told me that she had had to repeat for more than a month: « I forgive. » She had realised that when she said the Our Father, she did not really manage to forgive. And so she went and stood before the Crucifix and said, with regard to certain people: « I forgive you. » And she could not physically pronounce those words. So she began to shout, to forgive; at first physically and then spiritually. At the end of a month she was able to pray this sentence: « Forgive us our trespasses as we forgive those who trespass against us. »

You see that in prayer, you must live. Preparation for prayer brings us to prayer.

Our Lady says: « *Then you can ask for programmes. Inside your-selves, you can hear what God wants* – in yourselves, in a group – *and then ask for a blessing.* »

But the blessing Our Lady talks of is not mysterious, it is tangible. I discovered God's plan in prayer and so now I ask: « God protect me now and let this be accomplished. »

And we must accept this blessing and keep it carefully as if it were a pearl of great price. If we start from prayer in life, we force ourselves to live prayer all the time. End our prayer to enter into life, to accomplish prayer in life we come again into prayer. So we pray continuously. Prayer is valid insofar as we live it in our lives. And as we pray better and better, so will our lives improve and as life grows more and more in God, so our prayer improves. Try to say the Our Father in fifteen minutes, then in twenty minues, very very slowly, thinking about every word, praying.

You will soon see that certain sentences stand out.

I remember when, for a whole day I had to repeat the second part

of the Our Father, in particular: « Do not lead us into temptation. »
I felt so very weak, so limited; I had to shout « I am not capable
of walking here, give me Your hand, lead me forward, I am not
capable. » The second sentence: « Deliver us from evil »; I saw
that we are all immersed in evil and I began to shout: « Save us!
Save me, save the Church, save everyone because I can't go on
Father, You must deliver all our brothers. »
To pray, we must always open our hearts and at the same time – as
priests well know – do spiritual reading; real spiritual reading can
help us a lot to increase our prayer.

(Fr. Tomislav Vlašić - 10th April, 1985)

« Pray that hearts gripped by sin may open. I wish for this. God wishes it through Me »

I want to tell you the last messages and about the situation we are in. You know many other things from the television, from books and newspaper articles.

The apparitions go on happening every day with Vicka, Marija, Ivanka, Jacov and Ivan.

Mirjana has not seen these daily apparitions since Christmas 1982. Then there was one again on her birthday and on the day after, the feast of St. Joseph. She wrote to me, because she had the vision at Serajevo, and said that Our Lady gave her some new details about the secrets.*

Everything is still secret for us.

Our Lady spoke about those who do not believe, the atheists. She said to Mirjana: *« They are my children too and I suffer much because of them. If they only knew what would happen to them if they are not converted. Mirjana, pray for them. »*

Through Mirjana, Our Lady invites us to pray for those who do not believe. One could say that at Fatima, Our Lady announced atheism and said: fight against atheism.

Our Lady invites us to pray and to fast for those who do not believe. When we talk about atheism, we do not say we believe, but, in practice, are we not sometimes quite near those who do not believe, quite near atheism?

Mirjana also wrote that Our Lady took the Rosary from her hand and said: *« This is how to pray. Tell everyone that the Rosary is not just an ornament in the house. »*

So: pray. And Mirjana told me that some things are very near. But what does « near » mean for prophets? One never knows. A

* See page 115.

thousand years are like a day and a day like a thousand years. We must be careful and not think of dates, of days. Conversion is always urgent. It is dangerous to wait.

About Vicka, Our Lady ended by telling her the story of her life in Nazareth on the 10th April, it was Wednesday. On Thursday she told Vicka the date when it can be published and on Friday the name of the priest to whom Vicka must hand everything over.

Vicka did not tell me anything else, but she can tell the priest whom Our Lady named and he, on the day named by Our Lady, will tell everyone. We shall see what is written in those excercise books, the text which Our Lady dictated to Vicka.

Vicka said that the last thing was the introduction to the text.

She explained why she had told the story of her life; it was in answer to all the questions.

On Wednesday 17th, Our Lady started telling Vicka the future, the future of the world. After the vision, Vicka writes everything but cannot say anything. The situation is this; as from the 11th April, the visionaries see the apparitions in the priests' house, not in the chapel and they do not lead the prayers in church any more. Every evening one of them does the reading, or the psalm so that the pilgrims can see him or her.

As you know, our Bishop is still rather opposed to the apparitions. We have been asked to do these things. They are formal things. The statue, made according to the description of the visions, is now in the chapel, at first it was in the church. For us who believe, it is not very important who leads the prayer. The visionaries suffer because they are witnesses to these things. Our Lady needs these witnesses. Now, we have appealed to Rome because we must go on until the Commission has decided. And we are going on. At this time our Bishops are gathered together for the Episcopal Conference. I have no detailed news yet. They have discussed Medjugorje.

The Archbishop Franic seemed to me to be pleased when he came back. He spoke as a witness. Our Bishop also spoke. He is suffering for this and searching. His change of opinion shows that he is searching. At the beginning, he said in front of the whole Parish:

« If it were only one visionary, we could say: what does he want? But I have spoken to all six and I can see that they are sincere, they are telling the truth. Let us wait. »

Afterwards, he said it was all the work of the devil. So many people said that the devil has never asked us to pray, to fast and to submit to the Lord. And he stopped.

Afterwards, he said the visions were hallucinations, but the doctors said it was not possible, they were not hallucinations. He dropped this theory too. Now he says there is some manipulation. But I believe he will soon drop that theory too. I am convinced that one day these theories will become arguments for the authenticity of the visions.

It is like when St. Thomas said: Until I have... I will not believe. You know the story. St. Thomas did not want to believe that Jesus was risen. But he suffered...

I will tell you something. A Vicar General of one of the Italian Cardinals came in the name of his Cardinal. When he had seen everything, how we speak, how we explain the messages, who the visionaries are... (I think he also confessed a little...) he said to me: « Father, I feel that you are manipulating the whole thing, now you must tell me how it's done! » Can you imagine?

You also know of Prof. Joyeux's research.

All this research cannot be the last word concerning the apparitions. By a process of elimination, the doctors can say that it is not a case of hallucination, that it is not this or that. They will never be able to say that they see Our Lady. They can say: « We don't know how to explain it. »

There are many strange things. On Palm Sunday, one person said to me: « I saw a film sequence, the dance of the sun, for ten minutes. » One person has taken film with an American system. A Professor of physics and mathematics from Austria commented: « Inexplicable! » when he watched the phenomenon of the sun.

And the visionaries say that these are the signs of Her presence, they are a sort of advance sign of the great sign which Our Lady is to leave on the hill.

We do not know when.

The messages. Yesterday 18th April, Our Lady said: «*Dear children, today I thank you for opening your hearts, I feel very joyful for every heart that opens to God, above all those of the Parish* (all hearts then, also those in the Parish). *Rejoice with me. In all your prayers, pray for the opening of hearts which are gripped by sin. I wish for this. God wishes it through me. I thank you because you have answered my call.*»

Just a few thoughts.

Our Lady thanks all those who have opened their hearts, but at the same time, she also invites all those who are still burdened with sin, to prayer. At the same time she wishes to fill our hearts and oblige us to pray for the others. It is very important when she says: «*The Lord wishes it, through me.*»

If you read the interview with Archbishop Franić before Christmas, you will have found that, after Vatican II, mariology is once again at the heart of the Church. The Church will be renewed through Mary.

With the conception of Jesus, Mary was the first special bearer of the Holy Spirit; Mary is the Mother of the Church. She was the first Church, the first to believe in Jesus personally. The Jews believed in a Messiah, Mary believed in Jesus. And where there is belief in Jesus, there is belief in the Church. Beneath the Cross, Mary is the Mother of the Church and of all of us.

And theologically speaking, the renewal of the Church will happen through Our Lady who calls upon us to open our hearts and give thanks for every heart that opens and to pray that other hearts may open.

The message of last Thursday (11th April) was: «*Dear children, during this time, I want you to pray for enlightenment from the Holy Spirit. The Lord will give you more trials, difficulties and problems; but these are to strengthen your faith. Thank you for answering my call.*»

It is therefore important during this period after Easter to pray to the Holy Spirit. The Episcopal Conference is being held now and I believe that it is also for this reason that Our Lady has invited us to pray for light from the Holy Spirit.

We do this: every evening we pray for all the intentions of the pilgrims, of the sick, of parents and relations, but when She gives us the messages, then we pray chiefly for those intentions.

Now, until next Thursday, we shall be praying for all those who are still bound in sin.

On Maundy Thursday, she said: « *Dear children, thank you because you have begun to think of the glory of God in your hearts.* »

To think of the glory of God – what does that mean? It means searching for peace. The glory of God is not in the air, the glory of God is in us. If we search for peace, reconciliation and try to love everyone, to forgive; this is the glory of God.

And she said something else. She thought she would not give any more messages; this was the situation when our Bishop sent these new rules. But it is very important when she says: « *The Parish has acted, and so I will give you more messages.* » Here Our Lady demonstrates a very important point; the importance of the people of God as a people; the Church has all the hierarchy, but no one will be able to say: I was the one who saved everything. No one.

For example, a month and a half after the visions had started, the Parish priest was imprisoned, and the other priests and the nuns were within the parish, surrounded, the church was closed and cordoned off. No one could do anything, and the people of God came and prayed around the cordons, outside the closed church. And then it was opened again.

We must see our duty, yours, mine; we ask for the renewal of the Church. The Pope, bishops and priests can be, and are, servants when the people act. Each one of us is very important.

I believe that Our Lady leaves all these problems on purpose so that the people of God, who hear her maternal voice and follow her instructions through all the difficulties, can be seen.

So far we have no hierarchy to protect us with its jurisdiction, but we have many bishops and archbishops who can speak as witnesses, and it is testimony which will take us forward, not discussion.

Every cross, every difficulty is significant.

On the 28th March She said: «*Dear children, today I ask you to pray, pray, pray. In prayer you will find a deeper joy and solution to every situation which seems insoluble. I thank you because you have moved forward in prayer. Every one of you brings joy to my heart. I thank those who have encouraged prayer in their families. I thank you for having answered my call.*»

One very important thing. When She says: «*Pray and in prayer you will find a deeper joy and the solution to every difficult situation,*» I think that you will all want to ask the question: what prayer? How does one pray?

Perhaps one just makes the sign of the cross and says a Hail Mary to someone at the margin of our lives? Well, if one just says the Hail Mary or the Our Father sometimes, one cannot feel that deeper joy, but if we take time, if we listen, if we read, if we pray, then we shall feel that deeper joy. Each one of us wants that joy, no one wants to throw it away. We are all searching for it; it is characteristic of mankind.

We must ask ourselves if we want the means to achieve this joy. Our Lady asks us to say the Creed and seven Our Fathers, to recite the whole Rosary, read the Bible, go to confession and fast. All this is an exercise of preparation for joy, for love, for peace, for reconciliation. We must accept all that Our Lady asks as preparation of our hearts for what the Lord will give us.

In another message through Jelena She said: «*I am saved, but I wish you to be saved too.*»

That is why she invites us to prayer and fasting.

It is a programme for the whole of life and many of those who have been here have really begun with prayer and fasting. Every day we experience many graces; for instance, there are so many young people who never used to go to confession, who never prayed, and who come and are converted. The greatest grace does not consist in miracles, healing in the physical sense, but in moral healing, healing of the heart. And these are the fruits which will bring recognition by the Church.

In this sense, Medjugorje, as an event, depends on all of us, but in a positive sense if we go on doing all we are doing, praying, fasting and bearing witness.

(Fr. Slavko Barbarić - 10th April, 1985)

MIRJANA'S EXTRAORDINARY MEETING WITH OUR LADY
(18th and 19th March 1985) *

Mirjana Dragicevic, who is studying at Serajevo, had another meeting with Our Lady this year on the day of her twentieth birthday. The vision lasted 15 minutes. This is Mirjana's description of both meetings: « There were many of us. We went to wait for her at four o'clock in the afternoon. We all prayed for fifteen minutes and she was with us for fifteen minutes. She greeted me as usual with the words *"Jesus be praised!"* and I answered her greeting. She wished me a happy birthday and then we began to talk. First of all, she said how unhappy she was about the non-believers. Her actual words were: *"They are my children and I suffer for them because they do not know what awaits them if they are not converted to God. And so Mirjana, pray for them."* Then we all prayed together (She led the prayer) and said two Our Fathers and two Glory be's for the non-believers.

Immediately afterwards, she deplored the greed existing in the world and also at Medjugorje. She said: *"Woe betide those who are ready to take everything from those who come here* (to pay homage to Her), *and blessed are those who give."* We prayed for this too, saying two Our Fathers and two Glory be's. I prayed to be able to say Hail Mary's to her like this, and she smiled. Then we talked of the secrets, and I told her that I had a great many (about thirty) questions for Her. She smiled and told me not to worry about the

---

* Text in Italian displayed in the entrance of the Medjugorje Parish Church.

questions because when I came to answer them I would know the answers. She will give me this gift because to reply now would take too much time.

I asked her about Ivan... She said that the priests must be with us to help us because She has given us a heavy burden to bear and the priests' suspicions are hurtful to her. Then we recited the "Salve Regina" together with the others.

I forgot something. When She had blessed all the objects and I had taken them back, she asked me to give her the Rosary. She took it and started to pray saying *"This is the way to pray with the Rosary, you must tell everyone."* She said that one should not leave the Rosary about the house like an ornament as many people do.

On 19th March, she appeared again. The apparition lasted seven minutes. There were four of us. I spoke to Her about the secrets and we prayed. There was nothing else important to say. On both days She blessed us. »

When we say «pray» to the people, many do not know what it means

From the point of view of spiritual progress, Our Lady always calls to conversion, to prayer and to fasting.

When we priests speak of this, we come up against some problems. These messages are given along the way of spiritual progress, but many people do not know what we mean when we say «pray.» It means prayer but at the same time it means entering deeper and deeper into the heart of prayer.

For example, I have just finished with a class of thirteen year old children who are unable to find that peace and tranquillity. But when I made them say the Our Father as Our Lady had taught us we spent a whole half hour just saying the Our Father.

We can see that in every stage of our lives, if we pray in the right way, both children and adults are able to be quiet and are happy to be with God. I tell you this because, during the second week of Lent, Our Lady practised this prayer with the prayer group. And now I can tell you that if we want to pray well, we must live the Lord's Prayer every morning in a way that really touches us. The Our Father is enough to pray for the whole world, because He is Our Father, because in two words, we can embrace the whole world, both friends and enemies, as the sun shines on all, both good and bad. We must emphasize that in these messages, Our Lady told us that we have become so accustomed to our prayers. Prayer must not be a habit, but an inner need like the need to eat, not a need to pronounce words but a need to meet the Father, to meet God. If we pray like this, to meet God, to meet the Father, every prayer will make us happy, every prayer will change us.

If we do not feel this liberation, this happiness during prayer, then we have not prayed well; we have said the prayer but we have not met God, we have not met the Father. And to those who follow the rhythm of these messages, She brings us all to the heart of life, so people feel very very happy.

The other day a girl said to me: «I cannot get married now.» I asked «Why?» «I feel that the family binds me and I want to live in God, for God. I could accept a family life only if God were to say to me "Take this cross and bear it." I want to live for God.» This girl has had this inner experience; that with God there is life, whoever enters God finds life and the fullness of life. Now you can understand how people are able to pray day and night: they have found life. Now you can understand why people can pray in the fields, while they are working – they interrupt their work and pray – because they feel the need to pray, as they feel the need to eat or drink...

Our Lady brings us to this state of mind and there is no need to ask. What prayers? Our Lady's idea is this: to bring us to a state of humility, simplicity, sincerity and love. And in this state of mind, we should say the Our Father and the Hail Mary.

One Hail Mary or one Our Father is enough for us to live the whole day. There is too little time to say an Our Father, because if we enter into the depth of prayer, it will open out to embrace new meaning all the time.

For my part I will make this suggestion: go to Medjugorje and say every word of the Our Father, the Hail Mary with your whole heart; everything is wonderful when you enter into prayer.

It is enough to remember the words «Our Father, give us today our daily bread» and then you see that the world is crying out, searching and does not know what it is searching for. It is God who can give us bread.

«Forgive us our trespasses»: the poor nations are destroying themselves because they are so indebted and all mankind must be forgiven. We ask for this. When you enter into the Lord's Prayer, you can see that prayer brings you to faith and faith develops and opens every heart as a bud opens into a flower.

And now I say to you; Happy Easter, but not yesterday's Easter, the Easter you must live today, tomorrow, because now if you try to put into practice what Our Lady told us, very soon you will understand the importance of the apparitions after the death of Jesus.

The apparitions come as a necessary stage along the way to salvation. When we live what God offers us today, through Our Lady, we are able to be open to the time of the Holy Spirit.

Christians commit a big sin when they try to pray a little more or fast during Lent but when Easter Day is over, just let everything become empty. Easter lasts forty days and never ends.

And so I wish you a Happy Easter which may never end.

Every day I bring you to the Immaculate Heart.

Goodbye.

(Fr. Tomislav Vlašić - 19th April 1985)

Pray to the Holy Spirit for enlightenment

Those of you who have already been here several times, will see that we have transferred the statue of Our Lady which was made according to the description given by the visionaries, to the little chapel.

We did this because our Bishop wished it, he is as you know, still opposed to the events.

The apparitions come now in the parish house, but every evening, after the apparition, the visionaries describe what has happened and tell what they are allowed to tell and they always request a blessing for all those who are in the church.

We begin the Rosary at six and I beg you all not to stand in front of the parish house, as we might get into trouble.

We pray in church. One cannot go into the parish house because the room is very small. I ask you to pray with us. I will tell you when the visionaries begin to pray; we keep silence for a little while and then we sing: « Ave, Ave » or another hymn and we are all together.

Yesterday's message was very beautiful and calls us to work hard and constantly. Our Lady said: « *Dear children, today I want to say this; begin cultivating your heart as you cultivate your fields, cultivate and change your hearts so that the Spirit of God can live in your hearts. Thank you for answering my call.* »

Do you know how you should cultivate the fields to have good fruit and flowers? One must work hard and look after them every day. So it is with our own hearts; we must root out the bad weeds from our hearts and let the new Spirit of God come and live there. This is what Our Lady wants from all of us and this is also the meaning of the apparitions.

You know that we cannot expect new truths from the apparitions, but we can expect new stimulus and when people accept this, what God wants is already happening.

Our Lady did not appear so that we should begin quarrelling about whether she had appeared or not. The most important thing is to let ourselves be moved in prayer, in reconciliation, conversion, in fasting, in faith and in peace.

This is what Our Lady wishes.

And so I ask you never to forget this, for there are so many rumours, there are so many stories going round in the newspapers, in telephone calls, just do not forget this one thing: do everything Our Lady wishes.

If you have begun to pray here, go on praying and fasting in your own homes, in your families, do what Our Lady wishes.

Our Lady wants everyone's good and only our good. But I must repeat; the general message is always the presence of Our Lady. She shows herself here in a special and marvellous way and day by day, more and more people feel drawn here from all over the world. When we have understood Our Lady's presence through these events, then we shall understand that She is everywhere, always with us, like our Mother and, as Our Lord said, will always be with us.

From this presence, the other words and messages acquire a special and marvellous strength and this is the first and most important criterion for the apparitions if by appearing to the visionaries, Our Lady makes other people believe, and begin their conversion. After Easter, Our Lady gave this message: « *Dear children, I invite you to pray that the Holy Spirit may enlighten you. The Lord will give you new trials, but all will be allowed for the purification of your faith. Thank you for answering my call.* »

So speaks Our Lady and so did Jesus speak. This is the hardest thing for us all, the world over, and has always been in all times, not just today. There has always been·the Cross, there have always been difficulties.

And many have lost their faith because of their difficulties, and have asked themselves: « Why does Our Lady...? » But Our Lady says: « The difficulties are for our good, for the purification of our faith. » And I can say; it is true!

Here too at Medjugorje, we have always felt a great grace in all our troubles. Last year, when the Episcopal Conference forbade official pilgrimages, Our Lady said: *« Do not be afraid, allow yourselves to be guided. I guide everything. »* And it is always the same, even now. This month, I wrote in my diary; if there are fifteen hundred to two thousand people from all over the world every evening, this is a sign for all.

Our Lady arranges this if we listen, if we heed her voice, and you too are a sign that people, God's people want to see what is happening, to see these events connected with Our Lady.

So that after these events, no one will be able to say « I was important, I was the guide, I was the organiser, » no, because we have seen all along that Our Lady prepared every step through those who were ready to heed Her voice.

This is the most important thing for all of us, and for you who have many troubles, who are sick, or desperate, without hope; to search for the Will of God and live it, is the surest way through life, the way most full of joy even if you have to suffer.

In a message on the 28th March, she said: *« Dear children, I invite you to pray, pray and pray. In prayer you will find the greatest joy. »*

A question arises for all of us from this message; have we in our hearts a joy that we could call the greatest joy? If not, it does not mean that we do not want it, but perhaps our prayers are not yet the kind of prayers that will help us reach the greatest joy. Prayer is a meeting with God, with the resurrected Jesus. In the same way as all the Apostles were filled with great joy after meeting Jesus alive after the resurrection, so Our Lady calls us to this same joy, that is to meet Jesus.

After meeting a man, a friend, one needs time to understand what he wants, to tell him about myself. However, if our prayers only consist in an occasional sign of the cross, an occasional « Hello » to someone standing in a corner of our lives, the odd Hail Mary when we are tired, or when we are in some dire need, that is not the way to the greatest joy.

The trouble is this; we all want joy, but we are not willing to accept the means, to follow the path which leads to the source of joy, to the source of life, of love. This is the trouble, we do not want to use the means. And that is why Our Lady asks us so urgently and every evening to « *Pray, pray.* »

It is obvious that Our Lady is not asking us to waste time in prayers to find the way. When we reach a profound joy, we shall also have peace and shall be able to be reconciled with everyone.

When I tell you to pray, if you want joy, it is quite simple perhaps, but when you go back to your homes, pray reading the Bible, reading the Word, to hear the Lord speaking to your hearts and try to live these things. Then you will see that Our Lady is right when she calls you to prolonged prayer.

You know that she asks for the Creed, seven Our Father's, Hail Mary's and Glory Be's, the whole Rosary, and to read the Bible, celebrate Mass, go to Communion and make a monthly confession. When you say « It is a lot! », of course it is, it is a lot for those who have not understood the existence of prayer, but it is little for those who have met Our Lord resurrected.

And so I invite you; begin and continue as you can now, and always try to find the deeper meaning of prayer. Our Lady has also given us a marvellous means for doing this; and that is fasting. Many have confirmed that they are able to pray more deeply and easily when they are fasting. Our Lady does not call us to hunger, but to a process which comes about when we begin to fast; the heart is purified, we open out and can feel Our Lord better and so prayer helps fasting and fasting helps prayer and so we progress along the road to peace. And all of us and the whole world wants peace.

But when you are told to try to use these means, the answer is: « I cannot, I haven't time, I cannot work when I am hungry! »

If we Christians try to find excuses for not fasting because it is difficult, then perhaps we should think of all those who Our Lady calls her children and who are dying of hunger, and who have not got their daily bread. If we think of these things, perhaps it will be easier to take up these means for our own lives and along this road it will of course be easier to meet other men and easier to meet Our Lord.

(Fr. Slavko Barbarić - 26th April, 1985)

« You ask me to stay with you always, not to leave you, but now I ask you not to leave Me »

Our Lady appeared to bring us to prayer, reconciliation, to peace and conversion, to fasting and monthly Confession. This is what she wishes, and if you have begun and if you go on, this is already a recognition; that of the people of God; in fact you know, one does not pray by decree. Here one can see a church being born and suffering in birth, which is being born everywhere. The Church is born where you began to pray, with a group or with your family. And if you have begun and go on praying, you have already done much; this is what Our Lady wished. I told someone yesterday that I was cross because many stayed outside to look at the sun and the clouds. Our Lady did not ask you to look at the sun or the clouds at Medjugorje, she asked you to pray always; and I know that no one came to disturb the prayer; so I beg you, begin!

I know that you have prayed today, but when the evening liturgy begins, there is no excuse for anyone. I do not want to hear anyone I meet saying: « I have already prayed. » This is the Mass for pilgrims which Our Lady asked for.

She said: « *I want Mass to be celebrated every evening.* »

This is a special Mass with everyone; and that is why I ask you to help us; there must be silence in the courtyard too.

If you do not know how to pray, if you are tired, if you must smoke, go out of the courtyard. In this way all of us here become a sign of the faith, and of prayer. So I beg you to understand the responsibility of the message when you go back.

This is the situation and I know that Our Lady can win if she finds her people, her children praying, fasting, reconciled and trying to love.

Now I will give you some of Her messages.

The last message was one which will keep us hard at work all our lives: « *Cultivate and change your hearts so that the new Spirit of God can dwell there.* » A job for life. This is another word for conversion, also love, but above all conversion.

Root out every evil from our hearts. This is what Our Lady asks and you know how in a garden flowers and plants should be cultivated if we want the fruits; with patience and ever more patience. If a plant is closed and does not open to the sun it cannot bear fruit. If you don't put your heart into working in a garden and don't make the effort to pull out the weeds that choke the plants, you will have no fruit in autunm; to have fruit, a good gardener will even have to take a knife sometimes and in any case will have to do some very radical work and not leave even the smallest root of any weed that chokes the fruit-bearing plants.

And so one must not work superficially but deep down gradually changing our lives, our behaviour, our prayers, everything. This is the way to walk with Our Lady along the road to peace for all mankind, and we know that every man wants peace, wants to be loved, but those who are unwilling to take up the means of achieving peace are so many.

To want water and not want to go to the spring is illogical.

And if Our Lady asks us all to cultivate our hearts as we cultivate our fields; then don't wait! If you begin, the words of St. Paul are for everyone: « The Lord gives, after all, rain and everything needed for growth. »

The last message but one was this: « *Dear children, today I thank you for opening your hearts. I rejoice for every heart which opens to the Lord and especially for the hearts of the Parish. Say all the prayers for those hearts still burdened with sin, pray that they may be opened. I wish it, the Lord wishes it through me. Thank you for answering my call.* »

This is also a very beautiful message.

The Mother rejoices for every man, every son or daughter who finds peace, who begins to love, to be reconciled, who resolves conflicts. She is full of joy. At the same time she says: « *Pray that all may open their hearts.* »

Speaking on a human level, a mother suffers if her children live in conflict, do not love each other, behave selfishly and do not think of others.

This is again what Our Lady wishes, like cultivating our own hearts. In another message she invites us to pray for the light of the Holy Spirit and she said: « *The Lord will give you more difficulties, more trials, but all will be of use for your faith.* » These are the same words as those used by St. Paul when he said to all those who loved the Lord: everything will be converted to good.

This reminds me of a little message through Jelena. Our Lady said: « *You ask me to stay with you always, not to leave you, but now I ask you not to leave me.* »

When I looked at the date of the message, I saw that there were many difficulties at that time in connection with these events, and attacks in the newspapers.

Look how she speaks: « *You ask me to stay with you always, not to leave you, but now I ask you not to leave me.* »

One very important thing; when there are troubles and problems, do not leave Our Lady, do not abandon the Lord; all our trials are for our good.

These are some of the messages; I chose them as I wish, as I know that you are well informed and this replaces the sermon during the Mass which is celebrated in Croatian; so you will have food for meditation during Mass.

(Fr. Slavko Barbarić - 27th April, 1985)

In every prayer, we must express our inner life

As you see, when we listen to all the messages from the first to the last, they can all be summarized in those you have just heard: prayer, fasting, sacramental life, conversion and peace. But, what do these messages mean, the people really do not know. There are several reasons why people do not understand them.

The main reason comes from the very nature of the apparitions. The messages represent a whole pilgrimage with the people.

Those, therefore, who are near and who have been following these messages have learnt the depth of prayer, have felt what the peace of which the Blessed Virgin speaks, really means, they have practised fasting. And along this path, they have carried in depth, the words spoken by Our Lady. The messages have thus explained the various aspects of prayer, of fasting and sacramental life...

Briefly, the messages are: prayer, fasting, sacramental life, conversion and peace. These messages have, however, touched the very quick of men's lives. Ultimately, the Blessed Virgin wants to bring everybody to God.

A further reason is an interior one. Not everybody is ready to accept the level of the messages.

In order to explain this better: Last Saturday Jacov and Ivanka wanted to join the prayer group started by the Blessed Virgin through Jelena, as up till now they had not been able to join because of their school commitments. They now wanted to take part in order to share a deeper interior communion with them. But the Blessed Virgin said: « No. » She said: « You should now pray for a while with the Father, be well rooted in the way of spiritual life and afterwards you may join the group. »

I am telling you this just to explain how sometimes we are not always ready to accept the spiritual level on which the Blessed

Virgin speaks. I have noticed how we have in fact, held back Our Lady's messages; the entire Church, the whole world, even those responsible.

This restraint is simply the heart that resists, that rejects or does not progress as fast as the Blessed Virgin would like. Several times Mary told us what she wanted and how she had various plans for us: « *But you are not yet ready to accept them.* »

These then are the two reasons why people cannot understand the depth of these messages.

I am only saying this because all of you should try to progress, to be prepared for the messages because the messages from Mary cannot be learnt from reading the newspapers but only by words on a spiritual level. It all depends on the opening of your hearts.

And we are able to understand this at Easter time. Have you noticed three steps taken by the Apostles after the Resurrection of Jesus Christ:

– the first step: they saw Him but did not believe, they heard Him and still did not believe, they touched Him and were amazed; they saw Him but did not understand with their heart,

– the second step: is what we heard a week ago, when Jesus opened their minds, their hearts, so that they were able to understand all that the Messiah had said,

– and now the third step follows: you will now remain in prayer and wait for the Holy Spirit.

And when the Apostles had taken these steps they reached a state of total opening: a force from heaven had come; the Holy Spirit had enlightened them and so everything within them became clear. And S. Peter went out to preach with great authority because inside him everything was clear. This is, then, the course that the Church should take; we should also set forth with the messages of the Blessed Virgin: and enter into depth.

The main distinction of the last messages given to us by the Blessed Virgin through Marija who brings the messages to the Parish, is precisely the call in this moment to pray with sincerity to the Holy Spirit to enlighten the world, so that the light from heaven may descend upon us. If we really want to live these messages we must follow what the Blessed Virgin tells us.

We Christians make a great mistake: we practise Lent more or less intensely – we do something more by praying and fasting – but many empty themselves completely on Easter Day when they should, in fact, continue for forty days to experience the Resurrection of Jesus Christ within themselves.

There was no need for Jesus to come on this earth in order to be resurrected; He did it for us so that we could in turn experience our own resurrection. At Whitsuntide we can say that the Apostles were resurrected with the Holy Spirit, they underwent a change. These forty days should at least be as intense as those in Lent, full of joy, praise, and producing an interior flourishing of our spiritual lives. In the last message given to the Parish by the Blessed Virgin – it was that of April 25 – Mary said: « *There, the way you cultivate your vines, the way you work your fields and prepare the earth, this is how you should prepare your souls and your hearts for the divine grace.* »

By this I can explain to you how the Blessed Virgin follows two threads when giving the messages; one is the liturgy – this always follows the liturgic periods – and a second thread – meets us where we are and She usually uses images very near to the working person – and explains: do this, look at that, you must be open, you should do this or that...

Besides these two threads, there is a third that we cannot see, but that we can perceive by intuition through faith. The Blessed Virgin acts according to the mysterious events which are unknown to us but which await us, about which the visionaries speak in very guarded terms when they mention the secrets and the momentous happenings that await the world. These great events are close at hand and for this reason we are called to conversion, to a total abandonment to God; they call us and invite us to prayer so that we abandon ourselves to God.

Now, many ask the question: « How can I pray? » It is simple and at the same time complicated.

When we live a complicated life then it is very complicated, but for those who live a simple life it is very easy. I will give you an example which actually happened to me a week ago: it was the same situation of the prodigal son. After morning prayers when I was feeling very near to God, I had a lot to do, I had to go and work in another little church which we are building, my day was full... Problems regarding the little church came into my head and in the evening I went to pray, but was quite unable to. I needed a good half hour to settle down in order to pray. In the end I had to return home, as the prodigal son, in order to pray.

I then understood the situation in which the world finds itself to-day: we are all burdened with various needs and various pursuits. I then understood what Mary told us during Holy Week (Maundy Thursday): « *Try to rest in my heart. Do not stand beside me.* » God must not be next to us, nor the Blessed Virgin; but in our hearts.

But if we make little effort to pray deeply, God is not within us, he is beside us; perhaps even in just a corner of our homes, in a corner of our lives. Therefore, according to the messages of the Blessed Virgin, prayer means a great longing for God, a yearning towards God, an immense love of God...

As you all well know, when you have a good friend, then you can sit together for hours, one feels good, time passes... Now you see: it is also possible to be in prayer for four or five hours in such a friendly way that we feel good, really good... Until we do reach this state of friendship with God, we go to pray out of duty and not out of interior necessity.

When the Blessed Virgin emphasises: « *You cannot pray as a habit,* » every prayer should become something new, even an Our Father; you should express your life, express everything that is within you. Whoever has a great desire for God, to reach God, to live a true life in God, this person prays.

Many come to Medjugorje to pray for something, but not for God; to seek for something but not God. I want to live with God rather than be healthy, rather than be healed, rather than to solve this or that problem: I want to live with God, I want to live what is written in the Gospel.

So, he who earnestly seeks God is one who prays.

For this, we must be well aware of something. Lately, I was reading about some advice given to married couples by a psychologist. He was giving the example of somebody in New York, in the States.

A surgeon who was very absorbed in his work, sent his wife to a psychiatrist because she had become nervous; he then also sent his mother and ultimately his mother-in-law. The psychiatrist then called the surgeon and said: « You know, you dedicate too little time to your wife and that is the reason why she feels so frustrated. Every week you should take her to the cinema, be with her more and she will then feel better. » So the surgeon did this and felt very content, but the wife on the other hand did not get much better. So the psychiatrist called him again: « You have not understood me fully. I did not tell you: take your wife to the cinema every week, what I meant was: you must show love to your wife, you must find time for her, you must enter into her life and share it with her, only then will she be well again. » After this he said: « At last I understood what life was about and began loving my wife, my mother and my mother-in-law. I then had no more need for a psychiatrist. »

But these circumstances do not only apply to our human relationships. They also apply to our relationship with God. There are very many Christians who do their duty like that surgeon, but they are unable to go into depth in their spiritual lives, in fact they cannot progress in their spiritual lives. And because of this we see the tragedy of us Christians: after ten years a Christian is always the same, they do not grow in their spiritual lives. But why? They have not become aware of love, like that surgeon who afterwards understood what life was about, he dedicated himself to his wife and entered into her life.

Similarly, the Christian must enter into the life of Jesus Christ, to dedicate himself every day to Him and ask: what do you need, Jesus? What must I do for you? How can I promote your plans? How can I live in such a way that you may be resurrected in me? That you may be resurrected in my family? In my parish?

Now, if we put ourselves every day before Jesus with this desire, we will soon understand what we must do; if we dedicate ourselves at least a little more to our families, then we will see ourselves growing and will notice those around us rising again from a life, which we might say, is a life from the dead.

In my opinion this is the course which we should take if we want to make the messages of Jesus Christ become alive, otherwise, if we do not go beyond our duties we will not enter into the Kingdom of God. In the Gospel (Matt. 5): «Unless your righteousness exceeds that of the Scribes and Pharisees, you will never enter the Kingdom of Heaven.»

I would, therefore, like to tell you, from my own experience, this: go beyond your duties, approach Jesus with love, and with love draw near to the Gospel, to prayer and continue going forward until Jesus becomes your need, and when this happens you will find happiness. You will likewise realise that you will be happier with only half your material possessions rather than all you are presented with and not only this, but you will also find that your commitments will go more smoothly: as in the autumn of 1983, Our Lady said: «*Your work will not go smoothly if you miss your morning prayer; therefore, pray every morning and pray every evening. You must understand that your work cannot be done well without prayer.*»

I believe that many Christians chosen by God resist His grace. When God wants to send us crosses, through difficulties, we do not see the light any more, but whoever wants to go to the depth of Christian life must carry these crosses. A sick person who has an internal ailment cannot be cured until the medicine he takes, reaches the affected part. Spiritual progress is a treatment that God applies. I have often meditated on the conversion of the world and why God allows certain difficulties, certain crises, certain trials at Medjugorje: I came to the conclusion that it must be so and cannot be otherwise, because conversion is not a declaration but an act of healing of the organism of the Church, as in the case of treatment for an ulcer; it is necessary to open, to clean and to cure the organism. In general, and specially with those who want to progress in their faith, in their spiritual life, they very often resist their crosses and for this reason they cannot grow.

I also cannot forget the Easter greetings of Von Balthasar, received lately, who said: « Do not forget that every divine work must be purified through crosses. »
For this reason I am telling you that most people do not understand the graces and, in fact, show a resistance to them. I have also noticed along this journey of faith here in Medjugorje, that those who are not practising then stop as they do not go into depth, they do not discover the subtle meaning of the messages, whereas those who want to go deeply into spiritual life must ever improve. They, therefore, have to become capable of discovering precisely that subtlety of the grace; for if we want to build a house with walls of artistic workmanship, we have to look for experts, and it is the same in spiritual life.

You see that we all have to learn to pray because the messages have an educational role. If I say to people: « increase your prayer, » nobody increases it. But when I say: « let us say five Our Father's, » they all readily accept it.
I believe that the means of prayer given to us by the Blessed Virgin are simply instructions to get people to start praying. To enter into prayer does not only mean reciting the Rosary. In the prayer group guided by the Blessed Virgin, we only said the Our Father for the entire half of Lent. For hours and hours we only recited the Our Father and it was precisely the Blessed Virgin who wanted to bring us into the depth of prayer by saying: « *Better one Our Father than a hundred.* » Not in the sense of reducing the time for prayer, but in the sense of entering into communion with God through prayer. We must express ourselves and feel the presence of God: to truly reach this communion.
There are many forms and various methods: but they are unimportant. What is important, is to enter into depth.
But it is mistaken to think that we must pray only one Our Father

and that this is sufficient. We are able to pray one Our Father, only if we have first of all lived it.

In a message, after a group meeting, many members of the group asked. How is it that last time, last Thursday, when we practised the Our Father, we all felt a force, the presence of God, but when we got home and recited the Our Father, we did not feel this? – Blessed Mary replied: « *I will explain it to you: on Thursday you all went to Mass, you stayed for the Adoration of the Blessed Sacrament, you were filled and for this reason you were able to live the Our Father.* »

So you see, to live the Our Father, it is not enough just to pronounce the words, but to really enter into the content every day, deeper and deeper; both the meaning of the Gospel and of the Our Father must every day take on a new dimension.

I remember that one day, I needed to repeat: « forgive us the wrongs we have done, » because I felt the many many wrongs of the world towards God; « lead us not into temptation, » because I felt as a child that could not walk any more and I needed a Father to carry me along, because life was so complicated; I really felt incapable of going on any more...

I may say that we should express ourselves in every prayer and live the content of the prayer. Whatever form of prayer we follow is unimportant as these are only human usages as the Our Father is a usage of the Church, of the people gathered around Jesus. As you see, ultimately, to say the Our Father is to behave as a child before God.

Question: Is there any message to bring to the groups of Milan and Lecco?

Reply: Yes. That they go forward in prayer. This is a very important message because we are all inclined – this being a human weakness – to come to a halt as the Israelites did on their way to the promised land. And groups are inclined to tire or not to see the light, the guide-line necessary to go forward. Regarding this, it is extremely important to live a life of communion between groups and especially among those that are growing, to enable them to exchange experiences with each other; through this our eyes are opened and we are able always to go forward. It is dangerous to remain in a closed group. It is therefore necessary to live on this continual dynamic for the deepening of our prayer. But one must not expect anything exceptional of an exterior nature to happen, but only something that moves and develops within: that is, we open up ourselves more and more and are better able to understand the words of the Gospel. And in the manner in which our prayer moves, so also does the group move.

(Fr. Tomislav Vlašić - 29th April, 1985)

« I invite you to a more active prayer, and to participate in the Holy Mass. I would like every Mass to become an experience of God for you »

First, just a few words on the position of the visionaries, followed by the messages.

There are now four who see Our Lady every evening: Vicka, Ivan, Jacov and Marija. On 7th May Our Lady finished appearing to Ivanka. It was a Tuesday. They had all prayed together on Monday in the presbytery. Ivanka, Marija, Ivan and Jacov. Vicka was not well. They were praying in the presbytery and after a couple of minutes, which is how long the apparitions usually last, Marija, Jacov and Ivan uttered the word « Ode » as when Our Lady goes away, but Ivanka still remained in ectasy and Marija told me personally: « I was frightened because I could not understand what was happening to Ivanka »; as a rule Our Lady always comes and goes at the same time for them all. They stayed kneeling and continued to pray. Ivanka continued to see Our Lady; she stayed a further six minutes by herself and, during this apparition, Our Lady confided the tenth secret to her and finished telling her about the future of the world and of the Church (She has been giving her an account of this for approximately the last twenty-two months, beginning, I believe, on 9th June 1983. She then asked Ivanka to wait for Her the next day (Tuesday 7th May) alone at home. Ivanka did just this. The others came and prayed as usual in the presbytery.

Ivanka prayed at home and this apparition lasted an hour.*

Ivanka gave the following account: « The Madonna said to me: *"This will be the last regular apparition. I will come to you on every anniversary of the apparitions with the exception of the next*

* See page 145.

one (that is to say not in 1985). *You must keep the secrets I have confided to you closely, as well as all the texts. You can give them one day when I tell you to".* ». Ivanka confirmed that Our Lady again told her the date when she will leave the great sign but did not reveal anything.

Our Lady also told Ivanka: « *You must not think that it is your fault if I stop appearing to you. This was my Son's plan for you. Thank you for having followed all these messages and also for having given them to others. You have received a grace that not many people have had in the world. I know that you will be sad, but you must offer your sadness for the conversion of the world.* »

Our Lady then asked Ivanka if she had a wish and she immediately said: « I would like to see my earthly mother » and in that very moment, said Ivanka: « She appeared and I was able to embrace her. » Her mother told her: « I am pleased with you. » Then her mother disappeared and Our Lady remained. Ivanka describes her: « I have never seen her so beautiful, so splendid. She was with two angels who stayed all the time with her. » Ivanka embraced her and kissed her. Our Lady then disappeared. Ivanka was very sad after the apparition. Vicka said: « After the apparition she came to me and kept on crying. »

The next day I spoke to Ivanka and she gave me all these details concerning the apparition.

I asked her: « Well, you now know all the secrets, what should I tell the pilgrims? Hope or fear? » She replied: « Hope. The Madonna has come to save us. Pray. »

This is the position with Ivanka: she comes to Mass when she can. Our Lady gave her some personal advice. She did not want to tell me anything, so I said: « Tell me something so that I can help others. » She replied: « No, they are personal matters and I do not want to say anything. I have my own reasons. »

The position of Vicka is as follows: I have already told you that Vicka is ill: she suffers from headaches and rarely comes to church. She was here yesterday. Our Lady is still giving her an account of the future of the world.

Jacov, Ivan and Marija have no special task: During the apparitions, which usually last from one to five minutes, they pray with Our Lady for peace and ask for the blessing of all pilgrims and especially for the sick, also for the objects.

Every Thursday, Our Lady still gives the messages.

A word about Mirjana: as you know, Our Lady ceased appearing to her as from Christmas 1982 and promised to appear to her for her birthday, and so it happened also this year on 18th March. The apparition lasted about fifteen minutes and the day after about another seven minutes. Mirjana said that Our Lady had given her many details concerning the secrets but cannot yet divulge anything. She prayed and talked a lot about non-believers: Mirjana also cites a phrase from what Our Lady said: « *They are also my children. I suffer much on account of them. If they only knew what awaits them, if they do not convert themselves: Please pray for them, Mirjana.* » I would like to say two things about this message: firstly concerning this phrase: « *Mirjana, please pray for them* »; we must understand this and take it personally as if Our Lady had uttered our name. Secondly: who is an unbeliever? I should say that sometimes the non-believer can be found under our own skin. Of course, one can think of all those who do not know God, who say that God does not exist. Yes, these also. But there are also others who are very dangerous, who say: « I know God. I am a Christian, » but live as if they do not know God.

For example, when a Christian swears, when he gets drunk, when he harms others, when he lives in conflicts, when he does not want to come to terms with another, when he fails to take notice of the sick, this means that he is almost an atheist. So pray attention to your own atheism.

Mirjana said that Our Lady took the Rosary from her hands and said: « *Tell everybody, this is the way to pray. The Rosary is not an ornament for your house.* » So one must really pray.

Please do not stand in front of the presbytery during the prayers: enter the church, the priest will tell you when the visionaries begin to pray, as usual, a little before seven o'clock.

I wanted to bring to your notice one more thing as more and more pilgrims come here: as you have seen, there are many who come to market their wares here, to sell souvenirs and many other things. I beg you with all my heart, if you want a souvenir from here buy just a medal, a post card or a Rosary, but do not buy anything else. Why? If you start buying, then day by day we will see more stalls appearing: and we have to really fight against this. As soon as a coach arrives they run up with their souvenirs and one then loses the atmosphere. Many pilgrims have told me: « We are so glad there are not many stalls. » I say to you that if there is a market you have to be in two: one who sells and the other who buys. If you do not buy there will be no market. If you buy something to eat or to drink that is alright, but please not these things. If you still want to buy something you can go to Mostar or Liubuscki or somewhere else where there are these markets. I would be most grateful if you would tell also the others; sometimes I forget to tell you this. This is something apart, but none the less very important.

And now about the messages.

The first and most important message for everyone is the presence of the Madonna. Although Our Lady only gives the messages on Thursdays, every evening when she appears it is a message which we can put into words: « *I am your Mother. I am with you.* » And always, when she says to the visionaries: « *Go in peace,* » she is also saying it to us.

We can understand everything else that happens from this very presence. How, for example, this message has been spread in an incredible way. I was told that a small group in Mexico has distributed more than a million copies of a small book. They told me that already small groups were meeting. So the message of Medjugorje is spreading. This group told me: « We cannot find enough time as we are being invited everywhere for talks. » Many people are open to prayer and to fasting: Our Lady invites us to peace and many are thirsty for peace, we all want it. It is evident that there are many fully convinced people who want the truth; when we do not know how to explain these movements, many conversions, graces and healings, only Mary's presence can explain all. All this is a sign to us, a great gift, not only to this Parish but to the whole world and all Christians. However, you know that a gift is at the same time always a bond. So, if we have received we must progress and if we give to others that which we have received, everybody is recompensed. The role of conduct is what Our Lady demands implicitly of us: The Creed, seven Our Father's, the complete Rosary, the reading of the Bible, two days fasting every week and monthly confession.

Briefly: why the Creed? Our Lady has asked for belief. How does one begin to believe? It is a grace: all of us who have been baptised already possess this grace, but our faith can only grow if we dedicate ourselves to the Lord every day. Belief means to put your trust in God and not only to know that there is a God; this is what Our Lady asks of us, to take every day, indeed, a decision for the Lord. She asks for seven Our Father's so that nobody can make excuses: I do not know how to begin. It is very simple. But also in the number seven there is a completeness: the seven sacraments, the seven gifts of the Holy Spirit, the seven sorrows of Our Lady: therefore, always a fullness. To read the Bible, naturally is the Word which Mary had also known. And to recite the Rosary, well, this is a very simple prayer, meditative, biblical which one can alternate with periods of silence, with hymns and with words of praise; it is very suitable for the family where there are children because it is slightly rhythmic. In this way all those who know how to structure their Rosary can pray well.

Why fast? You can find a lot of reading on fasting, but I am telling you: just start. Fasting is like prayer, it is a duty for us Christians because both Jesus, Mary and all the saints fasted. And S. Francis, do you know how many days he fasted? This fasting means: living on bread alone for a whole day. This is very important, because one then gradually learns to live a simple life, one begins to realise that we have sufficient, that we do not have to worry and to be anxious and besides this it is also a help to resist our continual longing always to have more.

But the best thing to do is: start fasting and then you will see. But in order to fast more easily it is necessary also to pray.

Now, regarding monthly confession: this is obviously very important in order to receive the sacramental grace of reconciliation. In this context, I would just like to give you the last message, as it is of great importance: « *Dear children, I invite you to-day to a more active prayer and to participate in the Holy Mass. I would like every Mass to become a real experience of God for you. I wish to say to the young people: be open to the Holy Spirit. God wants to draw you to Himself especially now, during these days when you are coming closer to Him and at the same time when the devil is becoming more active. Thank you for having responded to my call.* »

This was last Thursday's message, that is of two days' ago. Why is it so important? I think that this message of Our Lady contains everything that she has said up to date. Why? What does a more active prayer mean to you, to me, to everybody? Each one of you should know by now how to pray. What happens in your families? Who is the one who encourages prayer in your family? Is it only your mother and the others let themselves always be driven along... I believe that we should be a bit active in the organising of prayers in our families. One should prepare a text from the Bible, another a word of praise, a hymn, another the introduction of the messages and yet another the Hail Mary. It is something formal but important because if it is always the same person, either mother or father, who has to take the initiative, there is the danger that he or she may tire.

Therefore, active prayer is the task for everybody.

This is only the formal aspect, but there is also the interior aspect for a more active prayer. When we pray truly with our heart, prayer does not become boring: who is active can dispel boredom and pray with zeal.

Keeping this in mind, the same can be said about praying with one's heart. So, I think that with regard to a more active prayer it can be said that we should pray not only when we are tired, when we have nothing else to do, but we must find time during the day in which we can be active; for if we pray only when we are tired there is the danger that we cannot become active.

Thus, step by step we can learn much.

Now, with regard to the participation at Mass, I am convinced, by examining both the experience of the Mass here and many other Masses with you, that people come at the last minute only when the bells rings and at the end they leave immediately. If they have found difficulty in parking as well, they are also a bit on edge and come into the church when Mass has already begun.

They may perhaps find some peace during Mass; but as soon as Mass is finished, they go. If you behave like this, there is always a risk: that the Mass cannot become in this way a true living experience of God; that is to say, one must prepare oneself.

Once Our Lady said: « *Come to church a little in advance.* »

From this I understood: leave time for a Rosary, twenty minutes beforehand in order to prepare oneself, and stay, say ten minutes, after the Mass is over.

For when you are teaching somebody you cannot say ten or twenty minutes is sufficient, but you must give time for the person to understand.

Once Our Lady said: « *It is sometimes better not to come to Mass at all rather than come in a hurry and go in a hurry.* » A priest once was quite shocked at this and asked: « How is it possible that Our Lady could say that it would sometimes be better not to come to Mass? » So I explained it thus: « Our Lady does not speak about the value of the Mass, but sometimes if we do not take part properly, there is the danger that we do not receive anything and, in the long run, if we receive nothing, one day we will no longer go to Mass. » Even in the kitchen where one prepares the best dishes, if one does not eat them one risks dying of hunger. The Mass is the centre of our lives and we must prepare for it.

You may perhaps now understand why we start praying an hour before Mass and why we stay for the seven Our Father's and for the prayers for the sick. As you can see, we prepare ourselves with the mysteries of the Rosary and consequently during Mass graces occur. I have seen that it is not so important to understand everything, but it is very important to pray in one's own tongue, meditate and then graces will come.

At Communion one says: « O Lord I am not worthy to receive You, only say the word and I shall be healed »; now, if we hurry away immediately after Mass, Jesus does not have time to heal our soul, when everything becomes just automatic.

Stay, therefore, pray, give thanks, always pray for your healing and for the healing of others in your own words. In this way the Mass becomes a live experience of God.

Thirdly, Our Lady told the young people: « *Be open to the Holy Spirit.* » This is valid for both the young and the old: in fact, I am telling you that as far as the soul and the spirit are concerned, everybody can feel young. If an older person succeeds in going forward in prayer, something in his life changes; he is young – on the other hand, a young person who says he cannot give up this or that, is already old in his soul, because he does not move forward. All of us, therefore, are young who let themselves move forward.

Another important thing: the Lord wants to draw us all to Him. When the Lord wants to draw us to him, He is as a father or a mother, He wants to grant us graces. It is true that we are somewhat used to running away from the Lord – I say this more or less in fun – If, then, we have no peace, no love, if we are always in conflict, this, I say is our own fault. The Lord is always wanting to give to us, but we run away, we say: « we have no time. »

One last thing about this message which is most important: the devil is very active. This is always evident. Wherever Our Lady grants many favours, there the devil is most active and tries to obstruct them. So, be on your guard: the Lord is really open to us, He invites us and if we open ourselves to Him we will receive in abundance.

(Fr. Slavko Barbarić - 18th May, 1985)

THE LAST DAILY MEETING BETWEEN IVANKA AND OUR LADY
(7th May 1985) *

On the previous day (6th May), Marja, Ivan, Jacov and Ivanka had the usual apparition.

The apparition that Ivanka had lasted eight minutes (six minutes longer than the others).

During these eight minutes the Blessed Virgin revealed the tenth secret to her and finished giving her an account of the future of the world.

She told her that the next day she would wait for her alone (this did not mean that the other visionaries were missing, but she appeared to Ivanka at home).

On the 7th May 1985 Ivanka had the apparition at home.

She said this to Fr. Slavko.

« As usual and as every day, the Mother greeted me with: *"May Jesus be praised"* and I replied: *"May He be praised for ever."* I had never seen Her so beautiful. She was so loving and so beautiful; her dress was magnificent and shone like gold and silver. Two angels were with her and they also wore the same dress. I have no words to describe all the beauty; those moments had to be lived. She asked me what I would like most at that particular moment. I wished I could see my earthly mother. She gave me a beautiful smile and my mother appeared; I saw her.

She was smiling. Then the Madonna told me to stand up. My mother embraced me and kissed me saying: "Dear daughter, I am so proud of you." She again kissed me and then went away.

Our Lady continued: *"My dear child, this will be our last meeting. But do not be sad as I will come every time on your birthday. Do not think that you have done something wrong and that is why I do not come any more. No, it is not that. The plans which my Son and I have, have been accepted by you with all your heart. The*

---

* Translated from the text in Croat displayed at the entrance of the Parish church in Medjugorje.

grace granted to you and your companions (the other visionaries) *has been granted to no other persons in this world.*

* *You should be happy as I am your Mother and I love you with all my heart. I thank you, Ivanka, because you have responded to my invitation and that of my Son; you have had much patience and have remained with us for as long as we wanted.*

* *My child, you must tell your friends that my Son and I will always be with you whenever you are in need of us.*

All that I have told you during these years, including the secrets, must not be revealed to anyone until I tell you to do so."

After these words I asked her if I could kiss her and embrace her. She did me this great favour. She blessed me and smiling, said: *"Go in peace."*

She then slowly, slowly went away together with the two angels. She was nearly an hour with me. »

There is a fundamental error: to ask for things instead of seeking God

The last messages tell us this: now is the time in which God gives us graces, we must pray and open our hearts; it must be emphasized that we Christians have forgotten the Feast of Pentecost, the Novena from which all other Novenas have come, the only Novena which is compulsory for all Christians and which is not practised in many churches.

We have heard in the messages of Our Lady, how important this period is. God is giving us graces, but these depend on our attitude to prayer and on doing penance. What I feel I ought to emphasize is, that many pilgrims go to Medjugorje and look for details and often they are more concerned about their personal problems but forget the very essence, and that is the main message for humanity. Only if we accept the main message, then will we find peace, we will find all that we are asking God for. There is a fundamental error: to ask for things instead of seeking God. He who is looking for things is not seeking God: he will find neither the things he is looking for, nor God. But he who seeks God will find both God and the things he is looking for, because Jesus said: « Seek first of all the Kingdom of Heaven and the rest will be given to you. » I stress this point because people who come to Medjugorje do not look at what the Madonna has said regarding all humanity, they do not pay attention to what Our Lady says, instead they look for something useful for their own lives. This is the mistake. And you cannot go into the depth of the messages of the Blessed Virgin nor into depth with the Gospel, if you do not seek this fundamental message.

Without this you can neither fast nor pray nor progress in your spiritual life. It is most important to keep all this before us: only then, little by little, will we understand things, we will see that God begins to take notice of our problems, but, firstly, we must be concerned with the problem of God, that is with what God wants of us. And this is the exchange of love that we must make. Now you cannot stop at one of the messages, for example, only the message on prayer, but you must follow every one of the messages. Whoever wants to go deeper into prayer cannot without also fasting. Whoever wants to understand fasting further and go deeper into prayer cannot do it without conversion.

So, here are all the messages, if we progress in depth, all together they form a single thing: I cannot pray if I do not change my mentality.

The world will not learn how to pray if it does not undergo conversion. If I do not walk on the path of conversion; if I do not fast, if I do not go deeper into my prayer, I will be unable to give up certain things, as I will not have the capacity of understanding them. If I am not detached from things I am not able to think. We know very well that when we are in love with someone we are also able to understand them. On the other hand, if we carry hatred in our heart we are not able to understand that person, but only to hate him.

And, therefore, if we wish to get to the bottom of the messages in our life, every day we must proceed, go forward, bestir ourselves on every level of the messages; that of prayer, of fasting, of sacramental life.

Once I said that I had seen many Christians who do their Christian duty, but I have seen very few who progress in their spiritual life. You can discover this truth for yourselves if you look around you: many people were just the same ten years ago as they are to-day. They have not progressed in their spiritual life, they do their duty, they go to church, they say their prayers, but do not go forward, do not change. And this is because of the lack of a way and the motive power of the Resurrection. And on account of this, we do not progress in our spiritual life, so the world cannot be changed. Only if I bestir myself, then people around me will move. But for this I must go forward in my spiritual life. The messages given by our Blessed Virgin during this period represent messages of a spiritual progression: whoever accepts these messages only as items of news or as rational formulae, has not understood anything.

The messages given to the Parish represent a whole journey.

In this way also the last message that the Blessed Virgin gave can be understood, when She invited all the parishioners to take part in the daily Mass. So you see the Parish is on its way, not out of obligation, but only out of love.

A group of Italian pilgrims asked me this question: « How is it that the people in Medjugorje are capable of praying for such a long time, hours and hours? »

In fact, there are girls and boys who sometimes pray the whole day during feast days.

I replied with another question: « But how can we live without prayer? » The people ask themselves this: « O my God, how many distractions keep me far from you: when will the time come when I will have all my time for you? »

Because with their encounter with God they have discovered the meaning of life. It is really while praying, while adopting the right attitude towards God that we become filled with the fullness of life within.

When we understand that we get more out of life by living with God, then our blessed life will begin; and we are all called to live this blessed life. We Christians should in the end understand that we are called to live a life to its fullness.

Remember when S. Peter said to Jesus: Look, we have left everything and followed you, and what do we receive? He gave as a reply: You will receive a hundred times more on earth and will be given eternal life.

By this, we must understand that every effort we make, every moment that we have offered for the Lord on this earth will be something useful for our happiness also here. If we go along on this level, then soon, God, prayer, fasting, conversion, will become something easy, something joyful on the spiritual level but not on the level of curiosity, and in this way we will be able to live the messages that we have heard from the visionaries. Otherwise, if we move only on the level of duty, we cannot go forward in our spiritual life and our duty will only become a burden. But if we start living these messages with love, we will soon discover that to live with the Lord is joy and in this way we will be able to bring the Gospel to others.

There then, the next time you go to Medjugorje I would like you to be happier and hope that we will all be very, very happy in Paradise.

I will always remember you in my prayers. Do not forget: with prayer you can move mountains. So try hard to change at least the half of your gossip into prayer; this will be sufficient to gain the Kingdom of God.

(Fr. Tomislav Vlašić - 19th May 1985)

« Remain in prayer and you will understand »

When pilgrims come, I always feel awkward. It is difficult to talk.
Let me explain: Our Lady only says a few words: *« pray, be converted, fast, abandon yourselves to God. »* We only have Her
messages, Her invocations. The Madonna only speaks a little and
we priests speak too much. I would like to be able to speak less
and have the power Our Lady has.

Another reason why I find it difficult to speak to you is because
you return from Medjugorje where you have already received all
the news. I also go from time to time to gather up the crumbs for
myself...

There is a third reason why I find it difficult to speak and that is
on account of the feast which we will be celebrating in a couple of
days: The feast of Pentecost.

In these days of the Novena we can recall how Christ's teaching
came to an end and still the Apostles were not convinced. At last
He said: remain in prayer and you will understand!

So as you see this third reason brings us precisely a deeper message
in the eyes of God; only by praying will we be able to understand
the will of God and Our Lady's messages.

I would now like to give you a thought. I will tell you what is dear
to my heart, and in this way you will be able to understand the
messages better and to pray better during these days.

In these last weeks I have felt a special message in my heart, during
the confessions of many pilgrims and more especially the Italians.
I must underline an aspect that many have forgotten, that many
have not even understood: Whoever goes to Medjugorje should
first and foremost accept the « kerigma »,* the message. Many

---

* « Kerigma » - acceptance of Our Lady's real personal appearance in giving
these messages.

pilgrims go to gain something for themselves, they think of their own problems, they ask for health at all costs, they look for an already planned solution. But this instantly blocks the conversion. It makes it impossible to move forward towards a solution which God opens up for us. When I said that the first thing to accept is the « kerigma » of the Madonna I wanted to emphasise this: one must accept that Our Lady has appeared. And this is a special gift for mankind to-day. She has appeared because sent by God. She has been sent by God to tells us many very important and urgent things for all mankind.

If, therefore, we seriously accept this, then all else will change; but if we do not accept this, it is as if we go on mending an old garment. You cannot gain salvation if you do not seriously accept this conversion to God.

I see two difficulties why people do not seriously accept the kerigma, the presence of Our Lady.

On a theological level there is, for me, a pretext when it is said: the apparitions of the Madonna are private and are therefore not binding. For me, this is a pretext. If a person is dying of hunger and another person comes who is filthy, extremely filthy, but offers the food to save the person dying, does this person take the food or not? We make an excuse also in the Gospel when Jesus speaks of the unjust tenants in the vineyard who beat the prophets. Finally God sends his Son. He thought that they would have let him free but instead they killed him also...

He now says: I will send my Mother: I also give you this blessing. When I reflect on the apparitions of the Madonna in the past centuries and even recently, at Fatima and at Lourdes, I ask this question to us Christians: have we seriously accepted the Madonna at Fatima or do people go to Fatima and to Lourdes just to ask for something for themselves?... If we had accepted the kerigma at Fatima and if we had accepted the message of Fatima, the world to-day would not be in this troubled state.

We have not accepted. We have treated the Madonna as a personal piety.

It was, instead, a message for mankind, for the Church. Also now

Our Lady is speaking to the world and therefore we must acknowledge her as a precious gift given to us by God, to be accepted and to be lived. And it is very important to understand that it is not a question of a general veneration of the Madonna. Here, we are offered a special gift, a special love, a special grace which we must accept in order to become filled with richness, in order to be saved. I reflected on this in the Scriptures and I saw that there were two possibilities for the world. One either the world is converted and saved or not converted and destroyed.

When the Israelites did not want to be converted, then Jerusalem was destroyed and they were exiled or killed.

If I am sick inside and do not want to be healed, how will I end up? I will die and suffer according to the extent of the illness. I only say this so that you can accept the presence of Mary and the message of peace for all mankind, the message of conversion, prayer and fasting. And you must accept it in earnest, as Our Lady told little Jelena during a conversation, in 1983: « *Accept me in earnest. When God visits his people it is for no light matter, but for very serious reasons.* » We must, therefore, seriously accept the presence of the Blessed Virgin, likewise the Scriptures, and then in our lives things will change. The illness will no more be a problem nor will the various crosses be a suffering, but instead it will become something sweet, as in the life of S. Francis when he embraced the leper and all bitterness became a source of sweetness for him.

And let us remember that passage of the Gospel chosen by Our Lady to be read every Thursday, Mt. 6, 24-34: « But seek first his Kingdom and his rightousness, and all these things shall be yours as well. »

We cannot have all these things before having sought the Kingdom of God. A plant cannot bear fruit before it is planted, nor can we receive the fruits of the Holy Spirit before being one with God, live with God and in God.

I, therefore, want to emphasise this kerigma: that is to accept the presence of the Madonna. If you seriously accept the presence of Our Lady, things will change. If you truly believe that eternal life exists it will become manifest through the presence of the Blessed

Virgin at Medjugorje. The visionaries have actually touched her, they see her and even hear her. A condition that can also be true for us. If we seriously accept this, our lives can change. But if we do not, then there will be no change within us.

I stress this point, as otherwise it would be useless going to Medjugorje: you would receive few fruits without this radical conversion, radical acceptance.

I have experienced this in confession during these last weeks, while talking to people in the confessional. I found that I was not able to help those who are clinging to the things of this world, to their health, to this or that problem; because they are not capable of listening to the priest when he talks, in order to bring the remedy to their problems. They do not want to change what they have already planned. God then cannot do anything because they do not want to change their attitude. I again urge you to seriously accept the presence of Our Lady and what she says.

I have another idea. The day after to-morrow is the feast of Pentecost. If, then, you want to be prepared for the feast of Pentecost you should seriously accept what I have told you and open yourselves. Do you know when a person is open to God? Not when he asks, but when he gives all, offers all. I offer myself to be changed, to do what you wish and not what I want, to demolish that which you do not like in me, to sacrifice my life for others.

The Holy Spirit is a gift, the charismas are a gift but can only be offered to me if I myself am a gift, if I want to live for others, if I really want to be a gift for others. Otherwise, I cannot receive it, because God does not throw gifts away but only gives to those who readily work and collaborate with Him.

As you begin to accept this kerigma, the presence of Our Lady and the messages, then you will understand that it is imperative to make your confession, to be converted, to abandon yourselves to God: I will give up everything. My pursuit is now God. If God becomes your main concern, then you will become God's concern.

This means seeking first of all the Kingdom of God.

Now begin reflecting: what does God want of me? What must I do for God? What can I do for you, at this moment?

We must truly reflect on these lines...

A fortnight ago, a poor woman with a child told me that she had left part of her field uncultivated. I asked her the reason why. I thought that perhaps she did not have the money to pay for it. Instead, she said she wanted to have a little more time to save at least one soul by praying.

Do you see? She left part of her field to save at least one soul! It did not come from a fanatical person. If you can see, it is the Gospel in its exact requirement: to leave your home, wife, everything to serve God. Do not leave your husbands, your wives, seek God and put yourselves at God's disposal. Live for God, also in your husbands, in your wives, in your work, and live for God.

There is a third point I am particularly keen to emphasize. Many good pilgrims, in fact I would say, very good ones who have accepted the presence of the Blessed Virgin at Medjugorje, and who believe, have put themselves more on an active level rather than a level to live the messages. This is a mistake.

There is a danger that the events of Medjugorje and the movement which has sprung from these happenings come to nothing. One cannot be active without nourishment.

I will read you a passage from the second letter of S. Peter in order then to make a reflection which might help you. When S. Peter invites us to live and to accept what Our Lord did and told us, he adds: « For this very reason do your best to add goodness to your faith; to your goodness, add knowledge; to your knowledge add self-control; to your self-control add endurance; to your endurance add godliness; to your godliness add brotherly affection; and to your brotherly affection add love. These are the qualities you need, and if you have them in abundance, they will make you active and effective in your knowledge of our Lord Jesus Christ. »

If, therefore, you have these virtues you will not be inactive nor ineffective in your knowledge of Our Lord: I would like to stress this, as I have experienced it in my life as a priest. Some wonderful movements have undergone a crisis when they tried to reach these fruits without this spiritual essence. Remember also the letter to the

Corinthians when S. Paul explains in depth what love is: it is necessary to really live love.

Before seeking gifts, even if they are very beautiful, one must seek faith. Without this spiritual essence the fruits become dry, often sour. Quarrels between people occur, they fight for ideas; instead of living with the divine strength they end by living by their own efforts, with human ideas: in this way one cannot bring God to others.

Everything that Our Lady has given us could be summarized in what S. Paul says to the Galatians: fruit of the Spirit is love, joy, peace, patience, kindness, goodness, faithfulness, humility, and self-control. The Blessed Virgin has invited us during these four years to live this spiritual essence.

Then the charismas given to us by God become alive, but without the fruits of the Spirit we are unable to bring the Gospel to others. The Madonna especially asked for peace. Activity brings us always to agitation and the Blessed Virgin says that all agitation always comes from satan. You must live in peace and if you want to progress in your spiritual life, on the lines of the message, then you must really try to increase your peace, and for this you will need silence and not to rush...

And in this context there are some beautiful messages. When Our Lady speaks to Jelena about peace she tells us how we should not think about the unpleasant things of the future but try only to bring hope within. This means: that you must be fully alive and to live the life of the Holy Spirit, of peace, joy, hope, patience, love and humility. In order to do this you must nourish yourselves before starting to run, because if you are filled with these gifts, only then will you be able to offer them to others. If I am empty, with nothing to offer to others, then I am only running.

Let me again summarise what I have said: Accept in earnest the Madonna and the messages, be concerned with God and God will be concerned with you. Seek the fruit of the Spirit before setting out in your activities. You must always be filled with the Holy Spirit and only then will you be able to develop the works, as Our Lady and as God want.

Yesterday I talked about being active. We have a certain experience, at least on a spiritual level; people have drained themselves and have been lacking in spiritual strength on account of the absence of prayer and the increase of their activities. I do not want to separate activity from prayer nor prayer from activity. However, the activity which we have to undertake extinguishes itself without the Spirit within us. We should work, I would say, more than others, but work with God so that each one of us is under the action of the Holy Spirit; do not act by the compelling power of human ideas, but by the strength of God.

I experienced this in these last four years when I was full of my own ideas wanting to save this person or the other and not succeeding in anything. When, however, I put myself into God's hands in prayer, only then did I see how everything changed.

In spiritual life there is a danger. I discovered it and I am afraid of this: that the person becomes the centre and God is left on the outside. The message I liked best that Our Lady gave were the words: « *pray, fast, let God act.* »

Actually I can do very little for mankind, but if I do my duty and entrust myself to God offering all to Him, so that He guides the world, then I can experience God omnipotent who leads the world. Do not think that I wanted to go against those who are active, by what I said before, but I know that many pilgrims who went to Medjugorje have become so active that they only pray for a few moments during the day and in haste. In this way, I believe, one cannot be a true messenger of God and of Our Lady. One can only be a true messenger if one lives the messages in their depth, and these can only be lived in depth if one prays more. This is precisely the reason why the saints went away into the desert. Also Jesus withdrew for forty days. And every night Jesus withdrew and escaped the crowd: He, who loved everybody, withdrew in order to be nourished so that he could carry on with His work.

I believe that spiritual life should have the same rhythm as daily life: day and night, that is rest, during the night and work during the day.

We have to be recharged in prayer and in our spiritual life, we have to gather up our strength to practise all that is sought of us as Christians.

One now can clearly see the role of the Madonna. What does the veneration of Our Lady mean? True reverence, true veneration of Our Lady is to act in the same way as the Blessed Virgin did in the face of God: to open ourselves to the divine Word, open ourselves to the Holy Spirit. Listening carefully to the messages of Our Lady in these days and particularly to what she says to the prayer group, these were all a preparation on the part of the Mother for her children to open themselves to God and to the Holy Spirit. Also those, then, who have not yet discovered the Madonna can understand that She wants their total opening to God. Our Lady is not a hindrance.

I must add another reason: with Our Lady you will go much faster towards God: it is a gift.

If you are able to live better without your mother in your families, then better send her away... but I do not believe it! The Church clearly said: the Blessed Virgin is the Mother of the Church.

At the end of May we will have this feast. I feel the need for my mother: I do not know how you feel. I have experienced, in spiritual life, that we are able to go more easily to God and to the Father with the help of Our Lady, with the help of our Mother; and during these apparitions I have discovered that the Madonna never wanted to hold a child tightly to herself, but always pointed towards God, she always brought us towards God and wanted to unite us to Him.

If you want to pray for me, I would be most grateful and if you wanted to pray to the Madonna for me I would be even more grateful. So please do accept the Madonna.

(Fr. Tomislav Vlašić - 24th May, 1985)

Seek first the Kingdom of God and all else will be given to you

Let us recite the third glorious mystery: the coming of the Holy Spirit. Let us try to recite it as desired by Our Lady. She has often repeated that one cannot pray well if one prays only as a duty. One prays well when one is seeking God, when one has a great desire for God. We will, therefore, try to recite this mystery as a real need from within, in order to encounter God, to desire Him, to feel every word we utter in our prayer, which we will now begin.

Be careful: it is very important that the words we utter are not words cried out aloud, but words spoken to our soul, in order to feel them within our being, to feel an interior resonance. And it is important to understand that only prayer can prepare us to understand the messages given by Our Lady. So let us begin with a hymn... Our Father...

It is usual that every Thursday Our Lady gives a message for the Parish. The last message of 30th May was the following: « *Dear children, to-day I invite you to pray with your heart. May prayer be for you, dear children, your daily nourishment especially now when you are exhausted by heavy work which prevents you from praying with your heart. Pray and you will overcome your tiredness. Your prayer will be to you both joy and rest. Thank you for having responded to my call.* »

There, Our Lady continues to give messages to the Parish, but the Parish is not only Medjugorje: the parishioners of Medjugorje are now spread throughout the world, and are in fact all those who want to follow what Our Lady says. Our Lady also gives us messages when we are approaching feast days, and for various needs and in this way She shows us the way we should behave, how we should live a life of faith.

I would like to extract what is essential in the messages and in the secrets from what all the visionaries tell us, and also from what they do not tell us, but what we can feel and hear. I wish to reflect specially on how the pilgrims who come to Medjugorje live the messages. Last week I told several Italian pilgrims that I thought that the centre of their behaviour towards God and towards Medjugorje had shifted.

At the beginning of the apparitions the people who came here were converted and there were in fact some very powerful and deep conversions. I asked myself the reason why this should be at the beginning, in such a deep way and why it does not happen now for everybody; and I found an answer in my heart and this during confessions.

The reason was because many had transferred the centre of their spiritual life: they had put themselves at the centre, and God and Our Lady on the outside, in the margin. This is what it means.

If we want to truly live and gather the harvest from the presence of the Madonna and of God, then we must accept the announcement of Our Lady and that which is essential. Many of you have heard and read about Medjugorje and the apparitions: many have come because they have heard of this miracle, these healings, or else they say: « Perhaps I too will be healed. » They then come for these reasons: this means going on the outside. Jesus said: « Seek first the Kingdom of God and all else will be given to you ». Therefore, you should put God and Our Lady at the centre.

The announcement of Our Lady is the following: Blessed Mary has appeared in this moment of time, sent by God, to tell all mankind some very important and urgent things. She has presented Herself to us and we must acknowledge Her.

Do you know what to acknowledge Her means? How would each one of you feel if you could embrace your mother, your father, your brother who were already dead? How would you feel if they appeared among you and said: « there exists a supernatural life and it is much more beautiful than life on this earth? »

To acknowledge Our Lady is to truly accept faith, death and the Resurrection, seriously.

160

Here Our Lady has manifested Herself: for the last four years the visionaries see her, touch her, hear her, listen to her: she has become alive.

If we seriously accept the presence of Our Lady, then our whole being will change. We cannot return from Medjugorje the same, each one of us, should it be the first or the fifth time, we must inevitably change, we must undergo a real change if we are to accept the presence of Mary, a being from beyond; and all the more so, when Our Lady speaks of the future of the world, and when she says she has come in order to tell us urgent matters concerning all mankind and in order to summon us. If we ask ourselves the reason why Our Lady is appearing for such a long time, She explains it by saying: « *These apparitions are the last ones for mankind* », so we must accept and seriously acknowledge Her. In 1983, in a message to Jelena, Our Lady said: « *Accept me seriously. When God comes amongst men He does not come lightly, but to tell them something of importance.* » So you see also this message emphasises the need to acknowledge the Madonna with Her message, genuinely and to put God and Our Lady with Her messages at the centre of our lives. At this moment, here in Medjugorje, it means this: seek first of all the Kingdom of God and all else will be given you.

In practice this means, that our main scope in life should be the annonuncement of Our Lady: this should be rooted in us. All of us should think well how to implement this. Ask yourselves: what can I do? How can I become a messenger of this announcement to the world? How am I going to talk about it in my family? in my Parish? how can I live it? This should be our daily concern. So, if we take the trouble to dedicate ourselves to God, He will unfailingly be concerned with us. He will solve our problems, but if we ourselves worry about our problems, we then leave no space for God to resolve them. Each one of us should, therefore, try to place Our Lady at the centre of our lives, with Her message, through prayer, meditation and through reading. To do this you do not have to read a lot of books on the apparitions of the Madonna both at Fatima and at Medjugorje; instead you should accept those simple words in the message: peace, conversion, prayer, sacramental life, fasting. It is sufficient to accept them, to live them daily and to deepen their understanding.

All the messages given to us by Our Lady in these last four years, can be understood better only through prayer, namely a great desire to accept God and His message, a great desire for God that drives us to pray. But those who want to pray and go into depth will find that they must change their life style, even in the family, in the Parish, because if they wish to truly live these messages, they will soon discover how all of us live sinfully. If, then, we wish to effectively go into prayer, we must change ourselves and that means we must be converted.

And we cannot be converted without prayer, fasting, without living a sacramental life, as Our Lady precisely pointed out several times. And as we progress on this course we will soon see that all Our Lady's messages become one, and that no message can go without the other. This is in practice for our daily life.

If you want to go deeply into these messages in your daily life, I suggest that you meditate every day also on the Gospel. I know that in practise in everyday life, when I do not meditate upon the Our Father, it becomes merely a routine, empty words. I utter them, but do not know what I am saying or to whom I am turning to.

Therefore, the meditation of the prayers that we say, that we recite, is precisely the condition necessary in order to bring us into the depth of prayer.

Yesterday, I told all those who came to Vitina that Our Lady taught us two steps in order to enter into prayer. They are the following: Firstly, to feel and recognize our sins before one's neighbour; if I have behaved badly in my family I must recognize this before my family, I must humble myself and when I have repented, I must accept God's forgiveness.

Now, this is most important: there are many who confess, but do not accept forgiveness. They continue with their thoughts and maintain a guilty conscience – it is therefore very important to believe in forgiveness. When we have accepted God's pardon we become freer to enter into prayer.

The next step is to offer all our worries to God, really leave them to Him, in order to be relieved of them.

If, every day we take these two steps in our prayer, we will enter into prayer in depth; our prayer, in this way, will not be something human, because the Holy Spirit will be free to work in us.

Only in this way will you be able to understand Our Lady's last message given to us on 30th May, when at the end She says: « *pray and in this way you will overcome your tiredness. Prayer will be to you both joy and rest.* » You see, this is because in prayer we must be redeemed and resurrected, namely, the resurrection of Jesus Christ in us. I recommend that you practise this in everyday life, both morning and evening: not, however, as a duty but in order that each one of you may be nourished, because the message says that prayer should be our daily bread. You well know how strong you feel when you have eaten and how you feel when you have not eaten for two days. Prayer should be a food: I should nourish myself in order to feel the resurrection, a strength within, so that my spiritual life, the grace, may be stronger than the evil surrounding me.

In order to understand better there is an important theological instance: it is often said that the apparitions of Our Lady are not binding, that they are of a private nature and are binding only to those to whom the Madonna appears.

I have repeatedly said that this is merely a rational pretext for if God says: « Here, besides all else I give you my Mother and send Her to you, » we are of course bound, not because Our Lady brings us something new which is not written in the Scriptures, but because She brings us the vitality of grace. You well know your mothers: seldom do they bring you something new, but every day they wake you up, they bring you your lunch and your dinner. Without this vital service you could die of hunger. God is sending Mary to us in this moment to grant us a special grace; acknowledge, therefore, this special grace; make this announcement known to others, so that people can accept the presence of the Madonna.

But when I tell you: « Be witnesses! », I do not mean just witnesses by word, but witnesses through the fruits that you are able to get by accepting the Madonna.

The main fruit which Our Lady speaks of is peace. If you are able to bring the divine peace in your hearts to men, without words, you will soon hear the question: « How is it that you are happy? How is it that you have such peace of mind? Peace within, instead of so many difficulties? » Before all else, we must live these messages of Our Lady, otherwise just to bring these words to others and not live them, means to change a movement or to transform a wish of Our Lady into fanaticism, because fanaticism is a movement of empty words or rather, an enthusiasm, but very superficial indeed without any depth, without accepting these fruits which She mentions.

And regarding this, I would like to stress something of great importance: when asking for graces, Our Lady always urges us to ask particularly for the graces of humility, sincerity, love, the gift of prayer and of fasting. This is very important: if you want to be true messengers you must begin from the bottom, from a behaviour of humility, of peace, of love, because during these four years we have come to understand that the root of spiritual life, as explained by Our Lady, is to be found precisely in simplicity, humility, love and the total abandonment to God. I shall never forget the words Our Lady said to me in moments of difficulty: *« Pray, fast, leave everything to God. »* This is what the movement to the centre means, when God acts in us, when we should not be worried, but only full of humility, full of peace, joy and love. On the other hand, when Our Lady told us about the temptations of satan, she gave us the necessary weapons not to let satan come near us: fervent prayer, humility and brotherly love.

So you see, if we have fervent prayer within us, humility, brotherly love and sincerity, it is impossible for satan to come anywhere near us, because there is no space between him and us. I, therefore, wish to emphasise this to all of you, if you want to follow this path and deepen these messages within you, try then to always live this fundamental attitude of love, peace, sincerity, humility and of a total abandonment to God. Then God will be the centre of your lives and not you! And God will look after you if you take the trouble to be concerned with Him. In practical terms: while you are here, start by going to confession, not because you are in Medjugorje, but because you want to start on your own conversion; if your confession is made without the perspective of conversion it is not a good one, as confession is something that binds us.

We take our decisions in our confession and have to follow them through. That is why I tell you: make your confession. But if you have confessed either yesterday or to-day you need not go to the priest, if you do not have any sins to confess; instead put yourself in front of God, and may this evening be an extended confession for you when you will experience in your hearts, a great de. e to carry out God's plans.

Again, another piece of advice: do not go looking for the visionaries. They are but a sign, an arrow that brings you here into the Church. During the apparitions we, here, have understood that Our Lady too has become like an arrow pointing towards God. Our Lady does not wish to hold us to Herself in order to keep us for Herself but She shows us the way towards God, She helps us to find God.

Therefore, do not go looking for the visionaries. You have here in church Someone greater than the visionaries, even greater than Our Lady: it is God. I would be very happy, and the Blessed Virgin would also be happy if you should have an encounter with Jesus this very evening. Christ will be given to you in a very simple way: « as food », you will be given everything. But as we do not receive the Lord in the Communion with faith, we are truly poor and Our Lady wants to lead us to this encounter with Jesus.

Please, then, come to Mass this evening: do not worry if you do not know the language. I would very much like to be for a week among people whose language I do not understand, to pray with them, only repeating: « O my God I love you » or « Jesus, I love you », with my eyes closed, because the language of the heart cannot be heard by the ear. You are thus in a favourable position if you cannot understand Croat. During Mass, enter into deep silence, with your eyes closed, and utter in your hearts: Jesus, Jesus, Jesus, Jesus. May Jesus be at the centre of your hearts, of your minds. Therefore, during Mass which will be in Croat (with a reading in Italian and possibly also some hymns in Italian), please try to participate actively.

And when I say participate, I am also thinking not only of those inside the church, but also those outside in the courtyard, because the courtyard is also the place where Mass is celebrated. Please do not smoke around the church or gossip, but be silent. Please help us to maintain this place as a place of silence.

The Rosary will begin at six o'clock: before each mystery a few words will also be said in Italian; at seven, Mass will begin.

The Mass is celebrated for you every evening, for all pilgrims and for peace in the world. So remember, that every evening Mass is celebrated here for you; when you are in your homes try to unite yourselves in prayer at this time, with those who are praying here in Medjugorje.

After Mass, seven Our Father's and Glory Be's will be said and we will invoke the Holy Spirit. And then prayers will be said for all the sick. But these prayers for the sick will only be effective and useful if you truly live the communion with Jesus Christ in the Eucharist. So please prepare yourselves.

Further, please do not go to the presbytery in search of the visionaries during the apparitions. Remember the words of Our Lady:

« *It is better for you to stay in church praying in faith, rather than be curious near the visionaries during the apparitions.* »

It is better for you to stay and to pray with faith instead of being curious. Besides, there is also a negative side to the signs which many people have seen: namely some of you start looking at the sun in order to see the signs. But I tell you to look at Jesus. Look at him in your hearts, seek him in your prayers: any signs that you may see do not last and you will eventually forget them all, but what is written in your heart will never be forgotten.

Therefore, look instead for the signs in your hearts, live the graces and you will be very happy. Lastly, I will tell you something: why do I tell you to accept the Madonna and to put her in the centre of your lives? I will tell you of my experience so that you may be happy, full of joy, of peace, and live life more to the full on this earth: do not forget what Jesus said: « blessed are the poor, blessed are those who are persecuted, etc. » If you begin to live what I have told you, you will begin to be blessed on this earth.

It is my wish that each one of you become blessed, so start this evening to be blessed, so that you may bring this beatitude into your homes and families, in your homelands. And may the message that you bring back to your parishes be the beatitude of your life. I give you my blessing.

(Fr. Tomislav Vlašić - 31th May, 1985)

May your prayer be the sign of your abandonment to God

Welcome. I know that you are well informed, also regarding the visionaries. I would now like to ponder on the messages.

The last message given yesterday and also the previous one have, I believe, the purpose of preparing us for the Anniversary. In the previous one She said: « *Dear children, in these days there will be people coming from all nations to this Parish, I therefore invite you to be loving. In the first place love your relatives and then you will be able to accept and love all those who come. Thank you for following my call.* »

This message has reminded us again of all that Mary wants from us: that there may be peace in our families and peace amongst all men.

It is another sort of peace, because peace without love, without the acceptance of others, of everyone, is impossible. It is therefore not just a problem of a world war: the problems begin in our families where there is no love nor reconciliation, where parents do not accept their children and the children their parents. Where one lives in conflict, there war starts: these are the most dangerous wars. Now one sees the importance of these words: « *begin by loving your relatives.* » You all know what dangers young people are exposed to when there is quarrelling in a family, for example, in cases of divorce. These cause almost irreparable damage and, therefore, when the message is accepted seriously, then it should really shake us.

So you see this is the condition. One cannot love somebody who is far away if one does not show love in one's family. We are bound to accept and love everybody, but we always have this love rooted in our families.

So Our Lady wanted to prepare us when She said: « *You are*

bound to accept and to love all those in the Parish, all who come to you. » But I say to you, it is essential to begin with your family: in this way, when we meet, we will have no problems.

This is yesterday's message: « *Dear children, I am inviting the people of this Parish to pray on this anniversary and may your prayer be a sign of your abandonment to God. Dear children, I know you are tired; you do not know how to abandon yourselves to me. Please abandon yourselves wholly to me. Thank you for having responded to my call.* » Now, when I think of this message and also of all the other messages and the spirituality of this place I would like to share with you some of my thoughts which may also help you.

When the Blessed Virgin tells us that we must pray, this is nothing new: She has repeated this invitation to prayer many times, almost in every message and more especially to Jelena. But there is something else very important and that is, that after Easter She invited us twice to pray with our heart. In one of these messages she said: « *I again invite you to pray with your hearts* »: and it is the same thing when She says: « *May your prayer be a sign of your abandonment to God.* » Prayer should be an encounter with the Lord.

We get upset if, when we talk to someone, they become distracted and do not listen. I am sure that you also stop speaking to somebody when you realise that they are not interested. It is the same during prayer: during prayer, the Lord wants to talk to us as he did with the two disciples of Emmaus, but if we are distracted and do not pray with our heart, nothing can happen. To abandon oneself and to pray with one's heart is the same thing. In these messages Our Lady has also mentioned one of our problems: « *Your hearts are still taken up by earthly things and they worry you.* » This is true: we cannot pray if many things worry us. For example, when one studies, if you are a little bit concerned about your exams, you can study well, but if you are very much afraid, you are completely seized with fear of the exams and cannot study. You cannot study because both your mind and your heart are distressed.

If there are trials and events that worry us so much, we are unable to pray with our heart: and so Our Lady invites us to be converted to prayer and to fasting. One frees the heart by fasting. I have much evidence of people who tell me: « When I fast I can pray better, it is easier and I can pray more deeply. » Therefore, if we want to follow the messages, to pray with the heart and to have the joy that prayer can offer us, then we see that we have to fast in order to be able to abandon ourselves to God.

In this message, Our Lady said: « *I know that you are tired* » and goes on to tell us the reason why: « *because you do not know how to abandon yourselves to me.* »

She said in a message after Easter: « *I invite you to prayer. Pray and you will overcome all tiredness.* » I think that you can interpret this as meaning also physical tiredness. For all of us, prayer should be a living encounter with the Lord, with Jesus Christ. He said: « All of you come to me and I will help you. » One can, therefore, also understand this message in a physical sense; we can also rest in prayer.

All those who say: what is the sense of living, of suffering? are tired. This is tiredness: and this message shows us that we can overcome it by prayer. From experience here, I can tell you: many who have begun to pray have been able to be reconciled with themselves, to find the meaning of life, of suffering and of everything else.

If we want to solve all our problems we must pray. In fact, before Easter She said in a message: « *Pray and you will find the greatest joy and the solution to all the most difficult situations.* »

Marija said that Our Lady has asked the prayer group to offer up to her, every Wednesday, even the smallest thing, every difficulty, offer everything to Her intention. Marija said: when we did this, offered everything to her intention, we immediately felt that our Blessed Lady had already taken these things and had offered them up to Jesus. We must offer everything to Our Lady including our sufferings, even our distress, our worries, our fears, everything, and then with prayer and fasting we will succeed more and more every day in this total abandonment.

(Fr. Slavko Barbarić - 14th June 1985)

« Abandon yourselves totally to Me »

... Only on Thursdays does Our Lady give us the messages and conveys them through Marija. Every evening the Blessed Virgin comes, greets us, blesses us, prays for peace and then goes.
This is the position with the visionaries.
In these days the apparitions last three to four minutes. The length depends on the Madonna.
The main message is the presence of the Madonna; even if She does not give us any message, She is in our midst and prays with us. The other messages have the purpose of directing us on our path: peace, conversion, faith, fasting and prayer.
Talking about peace, prayer, fasting and conversion, one can say a lot and books are being written on this theme.
Our Lady does not theorise on prayer and on fasting but invites us as when a mother begins to teach her child to take the first steps. She does not talk about the theory of taking the first steps, but takes her child by the hand, once, twice, three times until the child is ready to walk by itself. It is thus that all the explanation about prayer and fasting come to us as a service of the Church.
Therefore, rather than producing a theory on prayer, we must begin to pray if we want to follow Our Lady and if we want to understand the reason for fasting. Our Lady asks five specific things of us: every day the Creed, seven Our Father's, Hail Mary's, Glory Be's, the complete Rosary and the reading of the Bible, to fast two days a week and monthly confession. In particular I would like to say something about her invitation to fasting. She invites us. If, for example, one cannot fast, or if one does not want to fast then one does not have to go to confession because one has not fasted. It is an invitation of our Mother and all those who have heard and recognized our heavenly Mother in these events will do so, as they can.

I tell you that it is good to fast. Each one of us can fast and also pray.

Why the Creed and seven Our Father's? It is very simple. I believe that we should always understand this from an educational point of view. Our Lady has asked us for the Creed which is a decision we have to take every day.

The seven Our Father's are like a substantial prayer, but the number « seven » is also a symbol: the seven days of the creation, the seven sacraments, the seven sorrows and the seven joys of Our Lady; it is a number which has the meaning of joy and of sorrow. It is a substantial prayer. I can say that Our Lady has thought of something small so that nobody can make an excuse and say: « I cannot begin. »

If Our Lady had said: « Meditate for one hour a day », then many of you would have said: « I do not know how to meditate, I cannot. » So you see Our Lady does not theorise.

She then asks for the complete Rosary. Perhaps some of you feel like the person who telephoned me from Austria and asked me: « What does Our Lady ask for? » I replied: « The Creed, seven Our Father's and the complete Rosary. » He said: « What part of the Rosary? » « The complete Rosary » I replied. He again asked me: « What part? » I said: « No, the complete Rosary » to which he replied: « Who can recite this? »

It may seem a lot, but once you begin, it is not much.

Why does the Blessed Virgin ask for the complete Rosary? The Rosary is the traditional prayer well rooted in the Church. This prayer is a biblical prayer, meditative and has a special purpose to bring us nearer to Christ, meditating the mysteries of His life and of the life of the Blessed Virgin.

Here we see the teaching of Our Lady: by meditating on the mysteries of the Rosary we should get closer to Jesus. If the Madonna said: « Come closer to Jesus » many people would not know what to do, but when She says: « The Rosary » it is quite clear and I can begin. She said: « You must pray with your heart », and that is meditating, in such a way that the recitation of the Rosary brings us closer to Jesus and the life of Our Lady.

And, therefore, if we want to say the Rosary well, we must also read the Bible: then, every day, the Bible and the Rosary. I want to stress that if someone says the Rosary he must not live it like a Pharisee as illustrated in the Gospel: « I have recited a hundred and fifty Hail Mary's. » It is not a question of saying a hundred and fifty Hail Mary's, but of coming closer to Jesus. But I believe, the first steps to be taken are precisely to say the Rosary meditating it.

It is very important to remember the message Our Lady gave: *« I invite you to a more profound prayer, and to participate in the Holy Mass. »* She said: *« I would like the Mass to be a real experience of God. »*

She talked about the Rosary as a family prayer: it is well to know what active prayer means. I, therefore, ask you: who organises the prayers in your family? Who is active? Who says: « We now must pray. I have chosen a passage of the Bible, shall we read it? » Who turns off the television? Who unhooks the telephone in order to pray for an hour without being disturbed? If you do not disconnect these things you cannot pray in your families. Someone told me: « When I pray I am distracted. » I replied: « Look: do not expect that every day the Lord performs a miracle with your prayer. It would be a miracle to me if you prayed in a settled manner, because in order to pray well you should have a place, a corner in your home where there is a Cross, a Bible, an image such as a candle, in order to give light to the place. You have all studied and know that you cannot study in the dark. You must find a quiet place in order to study. It is the same with prayer.

These outward activities are, therefore, necessary for praying.

A few days ago – jokingly – people asked: « why do grandmothers exist in the world? » And the reply was: « in order to organise prayer. »

But if it were left only to the grandmother to organise prayer very often she may not know what to say. So be careful: I know of families where the father says: on Mondays, Wednesdays or Fridays you are responsible for preparing the prayers as you think fit, taking passages from the Gospel, choosing psalms and the hymns. And when one starts to pray in this way you will see that prayer becomes very important. If you want to become active in this sense: then organise your prayers. But regarding one's interior activity there is another very important message.

Our Lady said: « *Your hearts are still taken up with earthly needs, you are worried.* » If, then, something worries us a lot we cannot recollect our thoughts and therefore are unable to pray. Then our fasting will help us.

To sum up, we must deepen our prayer and prepare our hearts for praying.

I have much evidence of people who tell me: when I fast I am able to pray, and to collect together my thoughts more easily. Therefore one's interior activity produces an effect on the exterior activity. This interior activity has been asked of us several times by Our Lady, in other words when she said: « *pray with your heart.* » After Easter She likewise once asked us « *to pray with your heart.* » Why does Our Lady ask for so many prayers? She asks us to pray not in order to waste our time, but so that we may have joy. She said: « *Pray, pray, pray, for in prayer you will receive the greatest joy and find the solution to all difficult situations.* » You see there is no man who does not seek happiness, but there are many who do not want to pray, who do not wish to use these means in order to have this deep joy. You all know the story of the disciples of Emmaus, in despair after Good Friday. Their whole life can be summarised in what they said: « We had hoped: but all in vain. »

Think of those words. A stranger accompanies them and begins to talk to them and this stranger talks about suffering, about the Messiah and so they forget their worries and towards evening they say: « Stay with us. »

And when they broke bread with this stranger, they recognised Jesus.

If these two had said to the stranger: « Leave us in peace, we have our own worries, we are desperate », they would not have had that joy, that encounter which gives new strength. Therefore, to pray means to go along with Christ, to let Him act, to explain even suffering, difficulties and to sit down with him and break bread. If we just make a little greeting, a small sign of the Cross, we are unable to receive that joy which Our Lady speaks of.

In the message of 13th June she said: « *Pray and you will overcome all tiredness. I know that you are tired but the reason for this is that you do not know how to abandon yourselves to God. In these days abandon yourselves totally to me* »: This is valid for both physical tiredness and for that of the soul. In prayer one can find physical rest but the tiredness of the soul and of the heart is more important. You see, divorce in your family is a sign of tiredness, of not forgiving one another. For example, drugs are also a sign of tiredness.
Many are tired of life and of suffering.
This is a great sign of tiredness in the world. It seems that we do not have the strength of soul to forgive or be reconciled with one another, and Our Lady says: « *Pray and you will overcome all tiredness.* » Now, none of you wish to be tired in the soul or in the heart. Sometimes those who do not want to pray say: « Our Lady asks much too much time, I have to work. » There must be joy, in order to overcome tiredness and to obtain peace and thus be able to be reconciled. This is the purpose of our prayer: to open up to the gifts of the Holy Spirit. If we do not open up we remain without this reality.

The last two messages – you can also read them at the entrance to the church – should prepare us a little for the anniversary. In the one before last She said: « *I invite you to be loving, first of all in your families. Begin with your family and afterwards you will be able to love all who come.* » She added: « *In these days people will come to this Parish from all nations.* » Our Lady does not want us here to become Pharisees: that is to love the pilgrims but not love in our homes, to speak to the pilgrims about peace in one's work, in one's family...: « *Begin in your families.* »
This is also a message for you, too, to be able to love us, even when we have no time for you. You must begin with your families. You

can read about everything else and for the messages there is a book, « Open your Hearts to Mary Queen of Peace » of the groups of Milan and Lecco.

Here, I wanted only to give you a stimulus for praying and fasting. You will see what happens to you, if you will have listened and followed Mary's call.

(Fr. Slavko Barbarić - 15th June, 1985)

« Pray and you will be able to feel my presence »

Firstly: Welcome!

I propose to recite with you at least ten Hail Mary's in order to be ready to listen to what God says to us, because we are only ready to listen to what God tells us if we pray, that is, if we have made our hearts ready through prayer.

So, let us recite the first joyful mystery, how the Blessed Virgin received the message from heaven...

The last messages are characteristic of this. Our Lady invites us to prayer.

A very important message was given to the prayer group: Our Lady spoke to the group a lot about prayer during Lent, but after Easter only a very little. Why does not Our Lady speak? Perhaps She is angry with us? Perhaps we have not done all that Our Lady wishes? And everybody began thinking of this and that.

So the Blessed Virgin intervened by saying: « *I thank all those who are praying and feeling that I am present. I am sorry because there are some who say Our Lady is not in our midst. So pray and you will feel my presence.* »

This is the message: in order to feel Our Lady's presence you must pray; because the Madonna is not only present when She is visible, manifest, but She is always present.

This message brings us to reflect beyond the messages that Our Lady gives us. The prayer groups had to go deeper into prayer in order to understand in greater depth the messages given them during Lent, and also in order to understand what had not been said, and what the Holy Spirit can only say to the soul.

You see how Our Lady brings us towards the Holy Spirit and then leaves us again as a mother leaves her child to walk, to grow. We must discover this level of the Holy Spirit, which one meets through the virtues of faith, of love, of hope. A week ago a lady from the States was here with us. She was an Irish sister and in the past had had degenerative arthritis and had not even been able to move. She told me that on entering a little church she had been suddenly healed and received special graces: the grace of healing, the grace of a miracle, and the grace of spiritual discernment, the grace of faith in the sense of knowledge of the Spirit. This sister had come here because she was moved by the Holy Spirit. She had been given the specific task to come here and gather messages to take into the world. So this nun, after having been healed and after having received this grace has put herself at the service of the Church and goes everywhere, throughout the world, to guide the spiritual exercises of the priests, of the religious and also of the laity, but more especially to help priests to live their task, their vocation.

She also told us the story of her life: her mother died when she was very young and her aunt took her and looked after her.

When she entered the convent she always maintained a special affection for her aunt. When she was in Latin America to guide spiritual exercises for priests she received a telephone call from Ireland to say that her aunt was dying. Her superiors gave her the permission to go and visit her aunt.

She said that when she was about to take Holy Communion, she heard the voice of Jesus saying to her: « Who comes first, for you: I or your aunt? » She replied: « You! » « Then do not go to Ireland. » After which she said: « You are first, but my aunt is dying and I will not see her again. »

She again heard: « Who comes first? » « I or your aunt? » She replied: « You. »

After which, the sister told me she did not even want to telephone Ireland.

Several weeks passed and the sister was convinced that by this time her aunt would be dead. She afterwards telephoned a friend for news and was surprised to hear that at that very hour her aunt had been instantly healed. All the doctors remained surprised.

She then went to Ireland and visited her aunt and the Lord said to her again: « Did you think that you were more merciful than me? » She then said: « I understood everything from this voice: Did you think yourself to be more merciful than me? I saw my aunt and we said goodbye. » Her aunt then died in peace and full of joy. And this episode does not show that it is any ordinary story, but it is something sure and definite. I would like to ponder with you on this episode in order to understand who comes first for us.

It is really very difficult to say: we say in words that for us the Lord comes first, but in practice we see that many things come before the Lord: even our health, our home, our money, even our children, our wives, our husbands, all about which we worry so much, they distract us so much, this is why we do not have enough faith, enough love, all because we do not put God first. We are, therefore, unable to experience what the sister experienced when she heard: « You thought you were more merciful than me? » We can experience that the Lord is more merciful than we are and that He wants to make us happier than we ourselves possibly can; we can experience this grace of the goodness of God only if we put God first.

Let us reflect on the Gospel of to-morrow, on the readings; how merciful is the Lord: He makes the withered tree sprout and the green tree die; the smallest seed of the mustard tree becomes the largest by the work of God.

And while I was preparing for to-morrow and wondering what to say to the people, I understood something that I had not discovered before in the Gospel, the actual Gospel of to-morrow: I suddenly saw that we can be absolutely safe in the hands of our Lord, completely secure. But to be absolutely safe in the Lord, for us Christians, does not mean to remain passive, to wait: a 100 % safety exists but I must grasp it, I must achieve it and the Lord seeks my co-operation. It is on this point, in particular, that we should ponder if we are all that the Father says, if we really have done everything for the Lord. If we have done everything for the

Lord, then the Lord has done everything for us and we will feel all that the Lord has done, we will experience it in our lives.

It is a strange thing: when I tell people that Our Lady asks for the daily Rosary, they shake their heads and say: oh, who can pray so much, there is not the time; it is only for monks and nuns...

When speaking to some people I asked a man: « how many nights have you not slept? » He replied: « Two, one after the other. » Because he had been busy selling something, he was not worried for not having slept for two nights; half the people are awake until midnight because they have to water the plants or do something else, but are not worried. But when it is a question of praying, to be with the Lord for half an hour, most people are not capable of being with the Lord and they say it is too much.

But it is just on this point that we can judge whether the Lord is foremost or in second or last place in our lives; if, then, we experience that we have chosen the Lord to be foremost we will at that moment also feel his graces. We will not be able to feel those graces unless we have done everything for the Lord, and something will be missing.

You will not be able to understand Medjugorje without giving priority to the Lord.

For all pilgrims, Medjugorje will be transformed into just an outing if we do not put the Lord and Our Lady first in our lives. If we truly place God and Our Lady before all else we will then experience the grace, the immense grace that the Lord gives us. The last message that the Lord gave the group is an episode: Jelena saw the desert and in the desert a tree, above the tree a sun shining and the visionary immediately recognised Jesus Christ in the sun. And Our Lady also said: « *Many graces are granted to this group but you must not reject them.* » I would like to say to you and to all the world that there are many many graces which we could receive or either reject. It all depends on us as to whether we accept them or not.

We are ready to accept these graces only if we prepare ourselves through prayer, fasting and conversion: and this we must do every day. Every day we must give up something, we must again find the

180

Lord every day. And if we are on the way to this message shown us by Our Lady, we can then experience her presence together with the graces granted through Our Lady.

For those who go to Medjugorje several times, it is important to be sensitive to what is in your heart and be attentive, as Our Lady pointed out: « *Be careful of every thought. A thought is enough for satan to draw you away from God.* »

Whoever wants to serve Our Lady and progress in their spiritual life, every day must be vigilant to every thought, every influence flowing into their heart; they will in this way be able to progress in their spiritual life and at the same time discern between the divine spirit and the evil spirit, namely satan. And so as you advance in spiritual life, you will be able to guide others also.

Just in these days while talking to people, always within the spiritual field, we discovered that important movements in the Church came to an end precisely because they did not go more deeply into spiritual life in order to understand what the Lord wanted at that time, in order to pick up the finer meaning of the messages in the depth of their hearts.

Without discovering this level on which very very subtle divine messages are revealed, we are unable to go into depth.

(Fr. Tomislav Vlašić - 15th June, 1985)

If you want to discover love, you must go beyond mere righteousness

Greetings to you all. Welcome to this sanctuary. As I greet you I find it very difficult: all of you have come here and would like to be treated as friends, as brothers. It is necessary to have time for friends and all of you would like to meet one of us here, but it will be impossible to meet each of you individually.

We have therefore decided to pray for you and to follow you every day with our prayers.

So please excuse us if we do not have time for each of you individually, but we will follow you in prayer and do not forget that every evening the seven o'clock Mass is offered for you and for peace in the world.

I will now try to summarise the news and then go beyond this. I am sure you have not come here just for some items of news, that is of an exterior nature, but you have come rather for what is happening on a spiritual level.

There is nothing much that is new. The apparitions continue daily. What does Our Lady say to the visionaries?

Our Lady is the mother who awakens us, who calls us back again, who invites us. When we meet our mother every day there is nothing exceptional, it is an encounter with life, and so it is in all the messages that we have heard, there is nothing extraordinary on an intellectual level, but on a deep level concerning the heart, there is much that is extraordinary.

I will now tell you what is extraordinary.

At the beginning of the Novena for the anniversary of the apparitions, Our Lady told little Jelena: « *I do not want to reprimand people; if they do not want to see their own faults, then I will not mention them either.* »

You see, this is what is new. What is new can be found within our hearts only if our hearts are open, and if our hearts are more open, we can even receive more.

We see how God does not force our liberty; this is a sign of the supernatural nature of the events, because God always respects our liberty. He knocks at the door of our heart; satan enters by force and overthrows.

Like God, Our Lady knocks at the door and says: « *I am here, I am ready and are you ready to accept me?* » The same evening Our Lady said to Marijana: « *In the beginning you were like a flower, cheerful, full of peace, like a flower that had been watered well, but afterwards you became thirsty because you closed your hearts. So now I ask you to renew that initial opening.* »

On this point I would like to emphasize that we in the Church have a task to fulfill to-day: we all have a duty to be converted. Yesterday I met someone who began to say how difficult it was to acknowledge the apparitions. A peasant said: « Why, it is simple, one must go into the desert as John the Baptist did and fast and pray, then you will find that it is easy to see the supernatural nature of the events. There is no other path. »

And, in fact, if you want to understand Our Lady, make this evening a step towards the feast of to-morrow: talking is of no use. All the saints have had to tread this path. Without fasting and without deep prayer, without a total abandonment, where one forgets all and God is placed in the centre of our lives, one cannot find the interior light, the light of the Holy Spirit. I, therefore, call on you to begin your conversion this very evening: this also applies to those who have confessed this morning, because besides our own sins, and weaknesses, there are also the moments of weakness, the sins of the pilgrims as a whole.

There are certain things that I would like to mention concerning the pilgrims: I am also a pilgrim and we must reform ourselves. There is a point I would like to emphasise: many pilgrims have strayed from the centre of attention; many have read newspapers, books and watched television and have only aroused themselves to come here in order to gain something, to receive a grace, some health, to see something, and Our Lady has been put on one side. This is very dangerous. Our Lady, with her appeal, should be at the centre. The Blessed Virgin has appeared, sent by God to tell us at this time some very important and urgent things for all humanity.

I appeal to you to place Our Lady at the centre of your attention, both in theory and in practice. On a theoretical level, they say that the apparitions are something quite personal. From a theological point of view this is a pretext. If God has given us certain graces and tells us: «I am giving you another gift», then we are guilty, not by the rules but on a level of faith; by the rules, the priests of the Old Testament were right, but they had rejected the Holy Spirit and had sinned against the Holy Spirit.

Every grace that God offers us is binding. I, therefore, say to you: accept the Blessed Virgin, accept the apparitions of Our Lady; when I say the apparitions of Our Lady it is not the same as saying: «I believe in Our Lady» and «I acknowledge the apparitions of Our Lady» – it is different, because in all the apparitions of Our Lady in Lourdes, Fatima, and Medjugorje, we have been given special graces. If we are open to acknowledge these graces, we will be able to promote spiritual life in the world and in the Church.

On a practical basis it is very dangerous to talk about Our Lady and about the apparitions without living them.

I may tell you: on the 20th June Our Lady, through Jelena, told us how we should meditate on the Gospel and how we should meditate on these events: «*When a person passes through a dark tunnel and sees before him a light, we all follow this light. But a majority reaches that light and stays there in admiration. You, however, should go to the light in order to acknowledge it, to become that light, in order to bring it to others.* »

There, this is what is important: do not just talk about Our Lady, do not only admire, do not only look at the signs, but become the light for others.

In another message Our Lady added: «*When you take the messages to others try not to become completely empty. You remain*

deprived when you want to bring everything to the others at all costs; you will become completely empty. But you should carry the messages with humility, with sincerity, never forcing others; you should live in such a way that the others will be moved, awakened with the desire to live like you and not to defeat you.»
This is very important. Every day we should go on giving our testimony, and ever more deeply. To explain this better I think of a flower; in order to show its own beauty, its scent, it does not uproot itself to show you its roots, but its roots stay slightly hidden: the flower opens a little, sends out its scent, calls our attention to itself and, full of wonder, we receive its life. And in this way every Christian, every pilgrim, should be a witness similar to a spiritual flower fully rooted in God, and then with humility should give testimony, calling everybody to accept a life found in God.

A very strong message concerning the apparitions of Medjugorje – many pilgrims have forgotten peace. As soon as there is an article in the newspapers they lose their peace and start an argument, they begin to hesitate and give themselves to controversy.

Our Lady has told us several times: «*All agitation comes from satan*» and you should weather all trials with inner peace.

Now, referring to last Sunday's Gospel, there was the incident of when the Apostles were on the sea: a storm came and what did they do? They started crying out. But Jesus reprimanded them saying: «How is it you have so little faith?»

We should now look at this incident and meditate on it. There are three possibilities for us pilgrims: one possibility is to shout when we are in the midst of a tempest; this is also good, but not enough. There is the lovely possibility of longing for Our Lady, to feel ourselves filled with peace even during storms. If we have accepted Jesus Christ and his strength, his spirit, even in moments when He seems to us to be hidden, we will remain full of peace and we will be able to use that interior strength to control the elements.

I would like us to reach this point, by really praying and by weathering the storms around us, whether in the newspapers, in families or in the parishes; to reach indeed, such a close relationship with Jesus Christ that we feel within us the force to control storms always peacefully.

Now look, read again last Sunday's Gospel of St. Mark. Jesus only said two words and the storm abated. There, you must do the same. But you will only be able to do this if you reach a very close relationship with God, if you begin to feel as Jesus did, to speak as He spoke, to rest as He rested, to pray as He prayed and this means reaching that peace Our Lady speaks of.

There is a third group of the faithful who, when they experience the storm, do not even know that the Lord exists; they do not pray. And we all are a bit like this: think well, when there is a squabble in your families, the anger may last for hours and we still do not invoke Jesus.

This means to live without the Lord, this is to forget the Lord. When you are ill you do not say to the Lord: « Now what do I do? », you do not open the Gospel to see what the Lord says, how I should behave in this situation. You have this and that problem but you do not ask for the light so as to know how you must act. This means to live without the Lord: but I would like you to reach that attitude of peace, of which Our Lady speaks.

I beg of you, Our Lady told us that in times of temptation we must always remain in peace. Instead of using rage, one's own strength, or start discussing and arguing, Our Lady told us to pray very hard, stay calm, be humble, sincere, and with brotherly love. During these last months I asked several questions, through different visionaries: « what should be done in this or that situation? » They were very tricky situations and Our Lady always replied: « *You must love.* » You must love and all the rest will be easy. Once She said: « *You should love each and everyone and the Parish will be moved.* » She said to an American nun: « *If Jesus had had no love, there would not even be one Catholic to-day.* » It is love that moves people, that moves the world, it is love that nourishes people. For this I ask you to read the passages of the Gospel of S. Matthew (Chapters 5-6 and 7). Do not forget, if you want to discover love you must go beyond justice. We Christians often look for our rights, but our right is only love.

This year it happened to me that a father who had a daughter with an illegitimate child, came to me. At last the boy friend had decided to marry her and the father wanted to have the banns of marriage announced in church for his daughter's marriage.

But this is just not done with us, both in order to punish a little the transgression and also to protect others. The father was furious; he wanted the publication of the banns of his daughter to be announced at all costs. But then I also began to become angry and said: « But it is the rule of the Church », and that father went away from me, full of anger. I then meditated on this and understood that I had sinned. I had said « the rule. » But if that man was wounded by the sin of his daughter, he was in need of healing, he needed to be recognized by others, to be loved again by others and not to be rejected. I realized that I had replied on the level of mere righteousness but not on the level of love: I repented deeply.

I would like you to meditate on this and we will all discover that every day we are unfortunately men of mere righteousness instead of men of love.

To all those who have come here, and I hope for many it is the second or third time, I say, if you begin to read Our Lady's messages only just as they are written, you will not understand anything. You are invited to take the following steps, first to try to understand the very subtle contents of Our Lady's messages in your hearts. What does it mean to love? Every day we must discover it more deeply. If we are able to understand these messages along the path of our growth, then these happenings and this movement born here will bear fruit in the Church. If we only carry the written messages, just learnt by heart, we will not bring forth many fruits.

Lastly I say to you: tell everybody that we, here, love all those who oppose the apparitions. We bring love to all those who refute the apparitions. Tell everybody and, please, you too must love all those who refute the apparitions.

Those who oppose the apparitions have something that hinders them and they are in need of love in order to understand. They do not need discussions, fights, to take offence, they need love.

Tell everybody that we love everyone and we beg you pilgrims to love everybody, not to offend anybody, to love each individual, and to bring the peace of our Blessed Virgin as She has taught us. We are following you and everybody in the world, even those who are opposed to us, in prayer and love: you too, do the same.

Lastly, something very positive for all of you. We priests receive twenty-thirty-forty letters every day, but we are unable to reply to them all. You cannot receive an answer from Our Lady or the solution to your problem.

You are, however, invited to pray and to fast right up till the moment when you understand within, what God wants of you: for each one of us, the answer will be given by the Holy Spirit within us.

In the apparitions Our Lady has never spoken to anybody saying: « Do this and you will receive », but has only said: « *pray, fast and have faith.* » Consequently, pray, be converted and fast, in order to understand the will of God in your hearts.

If you are unable to understand, ask your priests. Read the Gospel and you will understand all.

And now let us all be converted: go to confession and be converted. That these days may be days of prayer: talk as little as possible and pray as much as possible.

(Fr. Tomislav Vlašić - 24th June, 1985)

The Father will do everything if we abandon ourselves completely to Him like little children

I wish to bring you into the depth of your hearts in order to understand the messages.

We have come to Medjugorje for a feast: The Queen of Peace. Our Lady wishes that every feast day should be the day of the Lord, not a day for tourism. Often She said that one should prepare oneself for every feast day: by fasting, praying, meditating. And on important Feast Days our Lady asks us to make a silent retreat. Our Lady calls us to an interior feast, to pray in silence.

Thus, once at Christmas two years ago, Our Lady said to Jelena: «*None of you have remembered to retire in silence to ask the Lord for His grace.*» Christmas can, in fact, often be a rather exterior festivity and the Madonna invites us, instead, to live it interiorly.

But when it is a question of feast days, according to Our Lady, and also as far as our Christian life is concerned – which, however, in a certain sense we have forgotten – every Sunday is a feast day. Unfortunately, we have turned Sundays into a day for tourism: one goes to a short Mass and one wanders round, one takes time off for tourism, but not to rest in the Lord. In order to celebrate, the Blessed Virgin invites us to prepare our hearts by prayer and with the sacraments. Here, in particular, Our Lady has stressed the sacrament of confession.

In the summer of '82 She invited us to confess monthly, but later She invited the prayer group and also the visionaries to confess every week.

Why did She invite them to confess every week? Because they had opened up more and could no longer carry the weight of their sins and because Our Lady wants us to grow continually. As to these confessions Our Lady wants to bring people to a total opening up of themselves. When a person wants to belong wholly to God, they have to go forward continuously and not tolerate even the smallest thing that might separate the soul from God. It is indeed along this path that we have discovered that all of us have a need to be guided spiritually: thus, it is not a matter of merely examining our consciences during these weekly confessions in a casuistic sense, but of feeling the real need to come closer to the Lord: and with this I would like to give you something really practical as to how you can celebrate and enter deeply into the spirit of the feast. Yesterday, little Jelena brought a message to Fr. Slavko; she had had a vision of a shining jewel which broke into two. Brilliant rays burst out and then, little by little, extinguished. The Madonna said: « *There, you see the hearts of those totally abandoned to God are like this brilliant jewel and when divisions occur, envies between people, little by little that jewel extinguishes itself.* » So, as you see, we must always be on a true path in our confessions and always sparkle instead of being extinguished. In order to do this I would like to tell you of a personal experience that I have come across, particularly in confessions with Italians: I discovered that during confessions many people begin by giving accounts of various incidents in their lives, the difficulties; but few ask for advice as to how to change their attitude towards these incidents. In confession, it is important to see our attitude towards events, suffering, difficulties. In confession, it is necessary to find a way to change our behaviour towards these difficulties or find the right attitude to adopt which brings us to salvation. I am certain that many people gain far too little after having been to confession because I have experienced, that after talking to the person, this person continues to talk about his problems: in this way, nothing happens and the confession does not bring us graces. In order to explain more fully: once Our Lady taught us how we should pray and said: « *Many Christians begin to pray but remain always at the beginning of their prayer and do not enter into the depth of prayer.* » In order to enter into the depth of prayer one must necessarily take certain steps. The first step is to confess one's sins and recognise them not only before the priest but, if I have offended a brother, I must recognize this sin before him and say: «Forgive me.»

This is the truth. If, therefore, I carry out this act before prayer, then I am capable of making the first step. In this first step it is important too, to receive forgiveness. But what does this mean? Many people make their confession but do not forget their sin. If it has been forgiven, then one must discard it, as otherwise we remain always resentful. And who judges us? Satan. Who condemns us? Satan.

We do not allow ourselves to remain under the influence of satan if God forgives us: we cast off our sin and begin to live our life again. Therefore, the first step to take is to cast off our sin and, in this way, we have taken a step towards interior freedom.

The second step: Our Lady tells us: «*Offer your problems to God.*» If you present your problems to God you have no need to tell them to your priest and to God. They are offered up to God and so you are able to pray; whereas, if you carry your worries, sorrows and tensions within, the Holy Spirit cannot act freely within you; you are a stumbling block for the divine grace. In order to enter into prayer it is necessary to cast off sin, we must offer up our worries to God.

Then, when we make these two steps we have reached interior freedom and the Holy Spirit prays within us, as Our Lady said in one of her messages: «*You must listen to the voice of God within, in each and every prayer.*» Thus, when we pray we ought to receive the answer to our prayers. If we receive the answer from God, then we are resurrected. For this I say: if you want to go to confession try, rather, to change your attitude towards the difficulties during this confession and this will bring you peace.

There is something else I wish to stress about confession: we Christians say that we believe in the resurrection of the dead, but we behave as if there were no after-life. I have met many people completely crushed, devastated because of a death in the family. But why be crushed when eternal life exists?

On the 7th May, when Ivanka had the last meeting with Our Lady, She asked her, among other things: « Have you any special wish? » The visionary replied: « Yes, I would very much like to see my mother » (her mother died four years ago). Her mother then appeared, embraced her and said: « I am proud of you. Go on serving God and Mary. » Her mother again embraced her.

You see, if we believe in eternal life, if eternal life is the foundation of our lives, then it is easy to change our lives. But if we do not believe in eternal life, we will never be happy in this world and never be filled with peace.

I, therefore, appeal once more to you to believe in the basis of our Christian life: death is our resurrection. If you accept these things and if you put them into practice you will produce great fruits and you will discover that spiritual life is not something apart, but is the root of our happiness, also on this earth.

Something else I would like to say to you and please do not forget it: I have words of discouragement that have come from Italy in these days; I tell you: « courage ». But courage in God! Do not forget: Medjugorje may go through trials, but not crises. I have been here three years and met with many trials: we, with our own strength could never have overcome any of these trials, but in all of them we have won because « God guides everything », as Our Lady told Jelena: « *When they make difficulties for you, do not complain, be happy and pray, because when God starts a work nobody will stop Him.* » I, therefore, say to you again: « courage » and « Live in hope. » Usually, when men encounter difficulties they react, they become aggressive or ful of fears; we do not have to become aggressive, nor be full of fears, instead, we must increase our hope in our trials.

And in your trials, praise the Lord, adore Him, praise Him, and if you are capable of praising Him in your trials, then He will solve your problems. This is the meaning of the Our Father: we are children and the Father does everything if we abandon ourselves to Him as little children.

I wish you all courage and to go on. The powers which we need are within us: we need only to awaken them by prayer, fasting and faith.

One last thing is this: on returning home please make some Christian resolutions because the most dangerous thing for us Christians to-day, for those of good will, is to allow ourselves to fall into an easy daily rhythm of life.

Decide then: This particular time of the day will be put aside for the Lord, when I will pray, my family will pray, as this time is dedicated to prayer.

If then, you make this time-table for the day, for the week, for the months, you will then follow your resolutions more easily and carry on the enthusiasm you have found here.

And lastly, one more thing, so that you are able to progress. God offers us many graces here, great graces; in order to obtain these graces there is no need to follow some extraordinary path. Our Lady shows us a very simple one. I say to you: start from to-day. It is asked of us to put into practice only that which we have listened to to-day, and that alone. If we put into practice to-morrow what we have heard to-day; the day after to-morrow the Lord will bring us a new light.

But if to-morrow we do not put into practice what we have heard to-day, we risk going backwards: thus causing a hardening of the heart. You all know the story of the sower, when a seed falls by the wayside, the birds come and take it away and the Lord says: « They are those who have heard and have allowed satan to take away the Word. »

See then: if you have come to-day to church and you have heard the Word but have then forsaken it, you have been robbed. You have been robbed by satan and you have come in vain.

Treasure the Word then, and put all you have heard into practice. If to-morrow you put into practice all you have listened to in the Gospel, and if you do the same the day after, you will see how grace will grow within you and will change the world. All those who are always seeking advice will not need so much counselling. It is a matter of listening. We are not capable of listening to the Gospel, of asking for the right answer. In the Gospel there is a clear answer for each one of us as to how we should change our behaviour towards our problems.

If there is this change from within, God will give us guidance, as often people who ask for advice do not really want it; they want something extraordinary and not something quite simple. They do not want to move on and therefore they ask for something extraordinary.

We priests can do little or nothing for those who have their ears blocked. Therefore, follow the path of Our Lady: the path of humility, simplicity, of listening daily to the Word. If you then decide and begin to do this, this very evening, you will feel the Grace of God. By doing this more graces will be given. On this special day, therefore, open your hearts in order to welcome the graces which the Lord offers you through the intercession of the Virgin Mary.

(Fr. Tomislav Vlašić - 25th June, 1985)

THE MESSAGES OF OUR LADY
TO THE PARISH OF MEDJUGORJE *

1st March, 1984

Dear children, I have chosen this Parish in a special way and wish to guide it. I will protect it with my love and wish that all of you may belong to me. Thank you for having answered my call this evening. I look forward to ever greater numbers of you joining me and my Son. Every Thursday I will give you a special message.

8th March, 1984

Thank you for your response to my call. All of you in this Parish, dear children, be converted. This is my second wish; in this way you will help to convert all those who come here.

15th March, 1984

I am particularly grateful also this evening because your have come, dear children. Continue the Adoration of the Blessed Sacrament. I am always present when the faithful are in adoration. This is the moment in which to receive special gifts.

22rd March, 1984

Dear children. I invite you this evening to honour, particularly during Lent, the sacred wounds of my Son which have been inflicted because of the sins of this Parish. Join me in prayer for the Parish so that His suffering may be alleviated.

Thank you for your response to my call. Try to come always in greater numbers.

* Text translated from the Croat.

29th March, 1984

Dear children. I urge you this evening to be particularly persevering during trials. Reflect on how the Omnipotent suffers to-day on account of your sins. Offer your sufferings to God. Thank you for your response to my call.

5th April, 1984

Dear children. This evening I ask you especially to honour the Heart of my Son Jesus. Think of the sacred wounds caused to the Heart of my Son, that Heart hurt by so many sins. Thank you for having come also this evening.

12th April, 1984

Dear children. To-day I ask you to stop all the tittle-tattle and to pray for the unity of the Parish, because both my Son and I have a special plan for this Parish.
Thank you for your response to my call.

19th April, 1984

Dear children. Have compassion on me. Pray, pray, pray.

26th April, 1984

Our Lady did not give any message.

3rd May, 1984

The visionary, Marija, asked Our Lady: « Dear Mother, why did you not give the message for the Parish last Thursday? »
To which the Virgin replied: « I do not wish to force anybody to do anything they do not feel or wish to do, even if I had some special message to give to the Parish with which I wanted to revive the faith of all the faithful. Only very few of you have accepted the Thursday messages. To start with there were many more of you. Unfortunately, for many of you it has become something quite common place and lately some were only asking for the message out of curiosity and not out of faith or devotion towards my Son and I. »

10th May, 1984

Many faithful appear to be struck by the last message of Our Lady. Some thought that the Blessed Virgin would not have given any more a message for the Parish, but this evening She said: « I will speak to you because I wish to tell you more. Try to pay attention to my advice. »

17th May, 1984

Dear children. To-day I am very happy as there are so many people who wish to consecrate themselves to me. Thank you. You have not been misled. My Son Jesus Christ wishes, through me, to give you special gifts; my Son is happy for your abandonment.
Thank you for your response to my call.

24th May, 1984

Dear children. I have already told you that I have chosen you in a very special way, just as you are. I, your Mother, love all of you so do not be afraid in moments of difficulty. I love you even when you are far from me and my Son. I beg of you, do not allow my Heart to cry tears of blood for the souls who lose themselves in sin; for this, dear children, pray, pray.
Thank you for your response to my call.

31st May, 1984 (Feast of the Ascension)

There were many people present. Our Lady did not give the message for the Parish and told the visionary Marija that she would give the message next Saturday so that it could be announced on Sunday during the 11 o'clock Mass.

2nd June, 1984

Dear children. This evening I wish to tell you that during this Novena you should pray for the Holy Spirit to descend on your families and on the Parish. Pray. You will not regret it. God will give you those gifts with which you will glorify Him until the end of your earthly lives.

9th June, 1984

Dear children. To-morrow evening please pray for the Holy Spirit of Truth, especially you of this Parish, because you need the Spirit of Truth in order to transmit the messages exactly and faithfully as they are given to you, without adding or taking anything away. Pray so that the Holy Spirit may inspire you with the Spirit of prayer, so that you may pray more. I, your Mother, tell you that you pray very little.

Thank you for your response to my call.

14th June, 1984

No special message was given.

21st June, 1984

Pray, pray, pray.

Thank you for your response to my call.

28th June, 1984

There was no special message for the Parish.

5th July, 1984

Dear children. To-day I wish to tell you that you should pray before you start any work and that you should finish your work with prayer. If you do so, God will bless you and your work. In these days you are working a lot and praying little. Therefore, pray: you will rest in prayer. Thank you for your response to my call.

12th July, 1984

Dear children. In these days satan wants to hinder my plans. Please pray so that his plan may not be realized. I will pray to my Son Jesus so that He may give you the grace to feel the victory of Jesus in the trials inflicted upon you by satan.

Thank you for your response to my call.

19th July, 1984

Dear children. In these days you have experienced the work of satan. I am always with you, so do not be afraid of the trials, as God always watches over us. I have given myself to you and share with you even the smallest trial.

Thank you for your response to my call.

26th July, 1984

Dear children. To-day again, I wish to invite you to persevere in your prayer and in penance; especially the young people of this Parish should take a more active part in their prayers.

Thank you for your response to my call.

2nd August, 1984

Dear children. To-day I am happy and thank you for your prayers. Pray still more in these days for the conversion of sinners.

Thank you for your response to my call.

9th August, 1984

Dear children. Please pray as satan wants to impede my plans again. Pray with your hearts and abandon yourselves in prayer to Jesus.

16th August, 1984

Dear children. I ask you in particular, of this Parish, to live my messages and to transmit them to all you meet.

Thank you for your response to my call.

23rd August, 1984

Pray, pray, pray (Marija says that the faithful and, in particular, the young people were called to order during Mass).

30th August, 1984

Dear children. The cross was part of the Divine plan when it was

built. Go to-day to the mountain and pray under the cross. I need your prayers.
Thank you for your response to my call.

6th September, 1984
Dear children. Without your prayers there is no peace. This is why I say: dear children, pray under the cross for peace.
Thank you for your response to my call.

13th September, 1984
Dear children. I still need your prayers. You will ask yourselves: why so many prayers? Look around you, dear children, and you will see how immense is the sin which reigns on this earth. Please pray, therefore, so that Jesus may win.
Thank you for your response to my call.

20th September, 1984
Dear children. To-day I urge you to begin your fasting with all your heart. There are already many of you who fast, more than anything else because everybody fasts, and so it has become a habit that nobody wants to break. I ask the Parish, please fast in order to thank God for having allowed me to stay in this Parish for so long. Dear children, fast and pray with your hearts.
Thank you for your response to my call.

27th September, 1984
Dear children. You have helped me with your prayers so that my plans may be fulfilled. Please continue to pray so that all my plans may be carried out. I commend all families of this Parish to recite the Rosary.
Thank you for your response to my call.

4th October, 1984
Dear children. To-day I wish to tell you that you have made me ever so happy by your prayers, even though there are still many

in the Parish who do not yet pray and for whom my heart is sad. Pray, to enable me to bring all your sacrifices and your prayers to the Lord.

Thank you for your response to my call.

11th October, 1984

Dear children. Thank you for having dedicated all your labour to God, even though He is now putting you to the test by the fruits that you are gathering in these days. You must know, dear children, that He loves you and is therefore testing you. You must always entrust all your burdens to God and you must not worry about anything.

Thank you for your response to my call.

18th October, 1984

Dear children. To-day I call you that you should read the Holy Bible in your homes every day. It should be placed in a prominent place where it can always be seen and where it reminds you that it « must be read » and accompanied by prayer.

Thank you for your response to my call.

25th October, 1984

Dear children. Please pray during this month. God has permitted me to help you every day and to defend you from evil. This is my month. I want to give it to you. You only have to pray to God and God will give you what you ask. And I will help you.

Thank you for your response to my call.

1st November, 1984

Dear children. To-day I urge you to renew your prayer in your homes. Your work has finished. You must now devote yourselves to prayer. Prayer should be at the first place in your families.

Thank you for your response to my call.

8th November, 1984

Dear children. You are not aware of the messages that God is

sending you through me. He is granting you great gifts that you do not understand. Pray so that the Holy Spirit may illuminate you. If you only realized the extent of mercy that God is bestowing upon you, you would pray without ceasing.
Thank you for your response to my call.

15th November, 1984

Dear children. You are the chosen ones and God bestows on you great mercy. You are not able to understand every message that I am giving you. Now, I only want to say: pray, pray, pray. I do not know what else to say because I love you and wish that through prayer you may be in a position to feel my love and the love of God.
Thank you for your response to my call.

22nd Novembre, 1984

Dear children. In these days you must live all the main messages and root them in your hearts until next Thursday.
Thank you for your response to my call.

29th November, 1984

Dear children. No, you do not know how to love and you do not know how to listen to what I say with love. You must be conscious, my loved ones, that I am your Mother and that I have come on this earth to teach you to listen with love and to pray with love but not forcibly, so that you can bear the cross. God is glorified through all men by the cross.
Thank you for your response to my call.

6th December, 1984

Dear children. In these days I call you to prayer in your families. In the name of God I have given you the messages many times, but you have not listened. This Christmas will be unforgettable for you, only if you will accept the messages that I am giving you. Dear Children, do not let the day of joy become a day of sorrow for me.
Thank you for your response to my call.

13th December, 1984

Dear children. You know that the time of joyfulness is near and that without love you will be unable to achieve anything. So, the first thing you must do is to love your family, all in the Parish, and only then will you be able to accept and to love all who come here. Dedicate this week, then, to learn how to love.
Thank you for your response to my call.

20th December, 1984

Dear children. To-day I am calling you to do something positive for Jesus. I would like every family in the Parish to bring a flower every day until the day of Joy, as a sign of abandonment to Jesus. I would like every member to place a flower beside the crib so that Jesus may come and see your abandonment to Him.
Thank you for your response to my call.

27th December, 1984

Dear children. This Christmas satan wanted very much to upset God's plans. You, dear children, must have felt the presence of satan also on Christmas Day. But God won in all your hearts. And may happiness reign in your hearts.
Thank you for your response to my call.

3rd January, 1985

Dear children. During these days the Lord has given you great graces. I would like, therefore, that this week be a week of thanks for all the graces you have received from the Lord.

Thank you for your response to my call.

10th January, 1985

Dear children. To-day, again I would like to thank you for all your offerings, in particular I thank those who are dear to my heart and who come here willingly. There are still many parishioners who do not hear the messages, but because of those who are specially dear to me, for their sake, I will continue to give the messages to the Parish. And I will still give them because I love you and want you to spread the messages with your heart.

Thank you for your response to my call.

17th January, 1985

In these days satan is perfidiously battling against your Parish. And you, dear children, have gone to sleep with your prayers and only a few of you go to Mass. Be strong in days of temptation.

Thank you for your response to my call.

24th January, 1985

Dear children. In these days you have experienced the grace of God through the renewals occurring in this Parish. Satan, always fiercer, wants to steal your joy from you. With your prayers you can completely disarm him and ensure your happiness.

Thank you for your response to my call.

31st January, 1985

Dear children. To-day I wish to tell you to open your hearts to God as the flowers of Spring seek the sun: I am your Mother and always want you to be nearer to the Father so that He may always offer many gifts to your hearts.

Thank you for your response to my call.

7th Fabruary, 1985

Dear children. In these days satan has been very much in evidence in this Parish. Please pray, my dear ones, so that the will of God may be done and that every action of satan may end in the glory of God. I have stayed so long in order to help you to resist the temptations.

Thank you for your response to my call.

14th February, 1985

Dear children. To-day is the day that I come to give you the message but not all the Parish accepts the messages and lives them. I am sad and would like you, dear children, to listen to them and live my messages. Every family must pray united and read the Bible.

Thank you for your response to my call.

21st February, 1985

Dear children. Day after day I ask you to renew your prayer in the Parish, but you do not comply. To-day I am calling you for the last time. It is now Lent and you as a Parish are now able to respond to my call with love. Should you not do so I will not give you the messages any more. This is granted to me by God.

Thank you for your response to my call.

28th February, 1985

Dear children. To-day I invite you to live, during this coming week, the words: I love God. Dear children, with love, you can do anything, even that which you may think impossible. God would like this Parish to belong entirely to Him. I too wish the same.

Thank you for your response to my call.

7th March, 1985

Dear children. To-day I invite you to renew your prayer in your families. Dear children. Stimulate the others to prayer and even the smallest ones to go to Mass.

Thank you for your response to my call.

14th March, 1985

Dear children. Each one of you have experienced the light and the darkness in your lives. God gives everyone the discernment to know good and evil. I invite you to the light which you must bring to all those who live in darkness. Day after day people who live in darkness come to your homes. Show them, dear children, the light. Thank you for your response to my call.

21st March, 1985

Dear children. I want to give you the messages and invite you therefore to-day, to live and accept my messages. Dear children. I love you and have chosen this Parish which is especially dear to me and where I love to be since Almighty God sent me. This is why I invite you, dear children, so that you may also have greater blessings. Listen to my messages.
Thank you for your response to my call.

24th March, 1985 (Eve of the Feast of the Annunciation)

Dear children. To-day I invite you to go to confession, even if you have already been only a few days ago. I want you to be able to live my Feast Day in your hearts, but you cannot live it if you do not abandon yourself to the Lord, so I invite you: « Be reconciled to the Lord. »

28th March, 1985

Dear children. To-day I want to invite you to: pray, pray, pray. In prayer you will discover the most sublime joy and the answer to all your problems which may seem impossible. Thank you for having started to pray. In my heart everyone is somebody special and I thank you who have encouraged their families to pray.
Thank you for your response to my call.

4th April, 1985 (Maundy Thursday)

Dear children. I thank you for having begun to think more of the joy of God in your hearts. It was to-day that I had intended to stop giving you the messages because some of you were not accepting me. But the Parish has acted, so I want to continue giving you the messages in a way that has never happened in history, from the beginning of the world.

Thank you for your response to my call.

11th April, 1985

Dear children. To-day I wish to say to all the Parish: pray in a very special way so that the Holy Spirit may enlighten you. To-day God wishes to put the Parish to the test in a very particular way in order to strengthen its faith.

Thank you for your response to my call.

18th April, 1985

Dear children. To-day I thank you for every opening of your hearts. I am full of joy for every heart that opens itself to the Lord, especially for those among the Parish. Rejoice with me. Pray so that the hearts which are under the burden of sin may open up. I so desire it. Through me the Lord wishes it so.

I thank you because you have followed my call.

26th April, 1985

Dear children. To-day I wish to say to you: begin to cultivate your hearts in the way you cultivate your fields. Cultivate and change your hearts so that the new Spirit of God may dwell in your hearts.

Thank you because you have followed my call.

2nd May, 1985

Dear children. To-day I invite you to pray with your hearts and not as a routine. Some of you have come, but do not want to go deeply into the prayer of the heart. As a mother, I invite you: pray so that prayer may prevail in your hearts in every situation.

Thank you because you have followed my call.

9th May, 1985

Dear children. You do not know what great graces the Lord gives you. You do not want to stir yourselves in these days during which the Holy Spirit is at work in a special way. Your hearts are concerned with earthly goods and these goods are troubling you. May your hearts be converted towards prayer and ask the Holy Spirit to descend on you.

Thank you because you have followed my call.

16th May, 1985

Dear children. I call you to a more active prayer and also to participate at Holy Mass. I want the Holy Mass to become an experience of God for you. I specially wish to tell the young: be open to the Holy Spirit because God wants to bring you closer to Him in these days when satan is very active.

I thank you because you have responded to my call.

23rd May, 1985

Dear children. I invite you specially in these days to open your hearts to the Holy Spirit. In these days, in particular, the Holy Spirit is working through you. Open your hearts and offer your lives to Jesus so that He may work through your hearts and strengthen you in your faith.

Thank you because you have responded to my call.

30th May, 1985

Dear children. I call on you again to pray with the heart. Dear children, may prayer become your daily nourishment, specially now that your work in the fields takes up so much time and you are unable to pray with the heart. Pray and you will overcome all tiredness. Prayer will be both joy and rest for you.

Thank you because you have responded to my call.

6th June, 1985

Dear children. In these next days men from all nations will come to this Parish. And I now invite you to love: above all, love your relatives and only then will you be able to accept and love all those who come to you.

Thank you because you have followed my call.

13th June, 1985

Dear children. From now until the fourth anniversary, I ask you to pray more in the Parish and to abandon yourselves still more in prayer to God. Dear children, I know that you are tired because you still cannot abandon yourselves to me. Abandon yourselves to me completely in these next days.

Thank you for your response to my call.

20th June, 1985

Dear children. For this Feast I want to say to you: « Open your hearts to the Lord of all hearts. » Give all your feelings and all your problems to me. I want to comfort you in your temptations. I want to fill you with peace, the joy and the love of God.

Thank you for your response to my call.

25th June, 1985

I invite you all to recite the Rosary. With the Rosary you will overcome all evil that satan now intends to inflict on the Catholic Church. May the priests recite the Rosary. Dedicate your time to the reciting of the Rosary. (Our Lady gave this message to the visionary Marija Pavlovic in answer to her question: « Blessed Virgin, what would you like to say to priests? »).

28th June, 1985

Dear children. With to-day's message I want to invite you to humility. In these days you have felt a great joy for all the people who have come here, and with love you have shared your experiences with them. I now ask you to continue in humility and with an open heart to talk to all those who come here.

Thank you for your response to my call.

PRAYERS

Prayer of Consecration to the Sacred Heart of Jesus *

Jesus, we know that You are merciful
and that You have offered Your heart for us.
It is crowned with thorns and with our sins.
We know that You implore us constantly
so that we do not go astray.
Jesus, remember us
when we are in sin.
By means of Your Heart
make all men love one another.
Make hate disappear from amongst men.
Show us Your love.
We all love You
and want You to protect us
with Your Shepherd's Heart and free us from every sin.
Jesus, enter into every heart!
Knock, knock at the door of our heart.
Be patient and never desist.
We are still closed
because we have not understood Your Love.
Knock continuously.
O Good Jesus, make us open our hearts to You
at least in the moment we remember Your
Passion suffered for us. Amen.

* Dictated by Our Lady to Jelena Vasilj, 28th November, 1983.

Consecration to the Immaculate Heart of Mary *

O Immaculate Heart of Mary, ardent with goodness,
show Your Love towards us.
May the flame of Your Heart, O Mary,
descend on all mankind.
We love You so.
Impress true love in our hearts
so that we have a continuous desire
for You.
O Mary, humble and meek of heart,
remember us when we are in sin.
You know that all men sin.
Give us, by means of Your Immaculate Heart,
spiritual health.
Let us always see
the goodness of Your Maternal Heart
and may we be converted by means of the flame
of Your Heart. Amen.

* Dictated by Our Lady to Jelena Vasilj, 28th November, 1983.

Prayer to the Mother of Goodness, Love and Mercy *

O Mother mine,
Mother of goodness, love and mercy,
I love you infinitely
and I offer myself to You.
By means of Your goodness, Your love
and Your grace, save me.
I desire to be Yours.
I love you infinitely,
and desire You to protect me.
From the depth of my heart I pray You, Mother of goodness,
give me Your goodness.
Let me gain Heaven by means of it.
I pray you, by Your infinite love,
to give me the grace,
so that I may love every man,
as You have loved Jesus Christ.
I pray You to give me the grace
to be merciful towards You. **
I offer myself to You completely and desire
that You follow my every step.
Because You are full of grace.
And I desire that I will never forget this.
And if, by chance, I should lose grace
I pray you to restore it to me once more. Amen.

* Dictated by Our Lady to Jelena Vasilj, 19th April, 1983.
** The phrase « I pray you to give me the grace to be merciful towards you »
means « Give me the grace to love your will which is different to mine ».

Supplication to God *

« O God,
our heart is in deep darkness;
in spite of this it is bound to Your Heart.
Our heart struggles between You and satan;
do not allow this to be so!

And every time our heart is divided
between good and evil
may it be illuminated by Your light
and made whole.

Never allow
two loves to dwell within us,
or that two faiths may ever co-exist,
and never allow to dwell amongst us:
falsehood and sincerity,
love and hate,
honesty and dishonesty,
humility and pride.

Rather, help us
so that our heart may rise up to You like that of a child,
Let our heart be captured by peace
and may it ever continue to feel nostalgia for it.

May Your holy will and Your love
find their abode in us,
that at least some times we desire truly to be Your children.

* The visionary Jelena Vasilj says that Our Lady dictated this prayer to her on 22nd June, 1985 and advised her to recite it in the prayer group.

And when, Lord,
we do not wish to be Your children,
remember our past desires
and help us to receive You once more.

We open our hearts to You
so that Your holy love may dwell in them;
we open our souls to You
so that they may be touched by Your holy mercy,
which will help us to see all our sins clearly
and will make us understand
that what renders us impure is sin!

O God, we wish to be Your children,
so humble and devoted
as to become dear and sincere children,
as only the Father
could wish us to be.

Help us, Jesus, our brother,
to obtain the forgiveness of the Father **
and help us to be good towards Him ***
Help us, Jesus,
to understand clearly what God gives us
because sometimes we give up doing a good deed
believing it to be a wrong. »

After this prayer, recite the Glory Be three times.

** Literally « to appease Your Father towards us. »
*** Jelena related later that Our Lady explained the meaning of this verse thus:
« So that He may mercifully make goodness come back to us and so make us good. »
It is the same thing as when a small child says: « Brother, tell Father to be good, because I love him, and so I too may be good towards him. »

215

Prayer for the sick *

O my God,
this sick person here before You
has come to ask You
what he desires, and
what he believes to be the most important thing for himself.

Grant, O God,
that these words enter into his heart:
« It is important to be healthy in the soul! »

Lord,
May Your holy will
be done unto him in everything!
If you wish that he be healed
may he be given health.
But if Your will is different
may he continue to bear his cross.

I pray to You also for us
who intercede for him;
purify our hearts
so as to make us worthy
for Your holy mercy to be given through us.

* During the apparition of 22nd June, 1985, the visionary Jelena Vasilj says
that Our Lady said this about the Prayer for the Sick: « Dear Children. The
most beautiful prayer you are able to recite for a sick person is really this
one! »
Jelena asserts that Our Lady declared that Jesus Himself recommended it.
Jesus wishes that the sick person and also those who intercede with the prayer
be entrusted into the hands of God.

216

Protect him and relieve his sufferings,
may Your holy will be done unto him.

Through him may Your holy name be revealed:
help him to bear his cross with courage.

_____

After this prayer, recite the Glory Be three times.

The Lord's Prayer

Our Lady teaches the Lord's Prayer to the prayer group* and wishes that this prayer be understood in this way:

FATHER

- Who is this Father?
- whose is this Father?
- where is this Father?

OUR

- this is your Father
- why are you afraid of Him?
- hold out your hands to Him.

.... (make a short pause)

OUR FATHER means that He has given Himself to you as Father, He has given you everything. You know that your earthly fathers do everything for you, so much more does your Heavenly Father.
OUR FATHER means: I give you everything, my child.

WHO ART IN HEAVEN

FATHER WHO ART IN HEAVEN

.... (make a short pause)

This means: Your earthly father loves you, but your Heavenly Father loves you even more. Your Father can get angry: He does not; He offers you only love...

* Through Jelena Vasilj.

HALLOWED BE THY NAME

In exchange you must respect Him, because He has given you everything and because He is your Father and you must love Him. You must glorify and praise His name. You must say to sinners: He is the Father; yes, He is my Father and I wish to serve Him and to glorify only His name. This is the meaning of « HALLOWED BE THY NAME ».

THY KINGDOM COME

This is how we thank Jesus and mean to tell Him: Jesus, we know nothing, without Your Kingdom we are weak, if You are not present together with us. Our kingdom passes, whilst Yours does not pass away. Re-establish it!

THY WILL BE DONE

O Lord, make our kingdom collapse, let Your Kingdom be the only true one, and make us realise that our kingdom is destined to end and that at once, NOW, we allow Thy will to be done.

ON EARTH AS IT IS IN HEAVEN

Here, Lord, it is said how the angels obey you, how they respect you; let us be like them too, let our hearts open too and may they respect You like the angels do now. And make it possible for everything on earth to be Holy as it is in Heaven.

GIVE US THIS DAY OUR DAILY BREAD

Give us, Lord, bread and food for our soul; give it to us now, give it to us today, give it to us always; that this bread may become food for our soul, may nourish us, may that bread sanctify You, may that bread become eternal.

O Lord, we pray to you for our bread. O Lord, let us receive it. O Lord, help us to understand what we must do.

Let us realise that our daily bread cannot be given to us without prayer.

AND FORGIVE US OUR TRESPASSES

Forgive us Lord our trespasses. Forgive us them because we are not good and we are not faithful.

AS WE FORGIVE THEM THAT TRESPASS AGAINST US

Forgive us them so that we too may forgive those we were not capable of forgiving until now.

O Jesus, forgive us our trespasses, we beseech You.

You pray that your sins may be forgiven you in the same measure as you forgive those who trespass against you, without realising that if your sins were really forgiven as you forgive those of others, it would be a very miserable thing.

This is what your heavenly Father is telling you with these words.

AND LEAD US NOT INTO TEMPTATION

Lord, deliver us from hard trials.

Lord, we are weak.

Do not let our trials, O Lord, lead us to ruin.

BUT DELIVER US FROM EVIL

Lord, deliver us from evil.

May we succeed in finding something worth while in our trials, a step forward in our LIFE.

AMEN

So be it, Lord, Thy will be done.

THE ROSARY OF JESUS

The Rosary of Jesus is in remembrance of the 33 years of His Life. In Erzegovina this Rosary was often recited, especially during Lent. In the past, the Rosary contained a specific passage which was recited for each year of Jesus, before the Our Father. In recent times, the recitation of this Rosary has been limited to the 33 Our Father's, the Creed, plus a few additions.

During an apparition in 1983 to the visionary Jelena Vasilj, Our Lady gave not only the form but also suggestions as how to recite this Rosary:

1. HOW TO RECITE THE ROSARY OF JESUS

a) *contemplate the mysteries of the Life of Jesus* helped by a brief introduction. Our Lady urges us to pause in silence and to meditate on every single mystery. The mystery of the Life of Jesus must speak to our heart...

b) *It is necessary to express a special intention for each mystery*

c) After expressing the special intention, Our Lady recommends us to open our hearts together in spontaneous prayer during the contemplation

d) for each mystery, after the spontaneous prayer, choose *a suitable hymn*

e) after the hymn, *recite the five Our Father's* (except for the seventh mystery which finishes with three Our Father's)

f) after this we must *exclaim*: « O Jesus, be strength and protection for us! »

The Virgin Mary told the visionary not to add or take away anything from the mysteries of the Rosary. It must all remain as explained by Our Lady. The following is the complete text which has been given to us through the little visionary.

2. THE METHOD OF PRAYING THE ROSARY OF JESUS

THE CREED

1st Mystery:

* Let us contemplate « *the Birth of Jesus* ».
  We must speak about the birth of Jesus...
* Intention: let us pray for peace
* Spontaneous prayers
* Hymn
* 5 Our Father's
* Exclamation: « O Jesus, be strength and protection for us! »

2nd Mystery:

* Let us contemplate « *Jesus helped and gave all to the poor* »
* Intention: let us pray for the Holy Father and for the Bishops

3rd Mystery:

* Let us contemplate « *Jesus trusted in His Father completely and carried out His Will* »
* Intention: let us pray for priests and for all those who serve God in a particular way

4th Mystery:

* Let us contemplate « *Jesus knew He had to give up His Life for us and He did so without regrets because He loved us* »
* Intention: let us pray for families

5th Mystery:

* Let us contemplate « *Jesus made His Life into a sacrifice for us* »

* Intention: let us pray so that we, too, may be capable of offering our life for our neighbour

6th Mystery:

* Let us contemplate « *the victory of Jesus: He has overcome Satan. He is arisen* »

* Intention: let us pray that all sins may be eliminated so that Jesus may re-live in our hearts

7th Mystery:

* Let us contemplate « *The Ascension of Jesus to Heaven* »

* Intention: let us pray that the Will of God may triumph, so that His Will may be done.

After this, let us contemplate how « *Jesus sent us the Holy Spirit* »

* Intention: let us pray so that the Holy Spirit may descend upon us.

* 7 GLORY BE'S TO THE FATHER, TO THE SON AND TO THE HOLY SPIRIT.